This book is lovingly dedicated
to *our* sisters and brothers:

Bailey, Brian, Cindi, Cory, Elishia,
Eric, Hylee, Jennifer,
Kimberly, Linda, Mark, Rick,
Shayla, Steve, and Taylor.

Chicken Soup for the Soul®
Celebrating Brothers & Sisters

CHICKEN SOUP FOR THE SOUL®

Celebrating Brothers & Sisters

Funnies and Favorites About Growing Up and Being Grown Up

Jack Canfield
Mark Victor Hansen
Dahlynn McKowen
Ken McKowen

Health Communications, Inc.
Deerfield Beach, Florida

www.hcibooks.com
www.chickensoup.com

We would like to acknowledge the following publishers and individuals for permission to reprint the following material.

Priceless. Reprinted by permission of Sandra Lynn Warner. © 1994 Sandra Lynn Warner.

Snake Attack. Reprinted by permission of Glady Bernice Martin. © 2006 Glady Bernice Martin.

Zip-a-Dee-Doo-Dah. Reprinted by permission of Wendy Greenley. © 2006 Wendy Greenley.

Got Raisins? Reprinted by permission of Glen A. Carlsen. © 2007 Glen A. Carlsen.

Terrified Together. Reprinted by permission of Renee Willa Hixson. © 2006 Renee Willa Hixson.

Payback. Reprinted by permission of Terri Kaye Duncan. © 2006 Terri Kaye Duncan.

(Continued on page 262)

Library of Congress Cataloging-in-Publication Data

Chicken soup for the soul celebrating brothers and sisters / [compiled by] Jack Canfield . . . [et al.].
    p.   cm.
    ISBN-13: 978-0-7573-0635-8 (trade paper)
    ISBN-10: 0-7573-0635-7 (trade paper)
    1. Brothers and sisters. I. Canfield, Jack, 1944–
    BF723.S43C433 2007
    306.875'3—dc22

                  2007020387

Publisher: Health Communications, Inc.
           3201 S.W. 15th Street
           Deerfield Beach, FL 33442-8190

R-09-07

Cover design by Andrea Perrine Brower
Interior formatting by Lawna Patterson Oldfield

Contents

3. STORIES SHARED BY YOUNGER SIBLINGS

4. STORIES SHARED BY OLDER SIBLINGS

5. LOVING HANDS

6. THROUGH OUR EYES

7. GOLDEN TIMES

8. INSIGHTS AND LESSONS

Acknowledgments

We wish to express our heartfelt gratitude to the following people who helped make this book possible.

Our families, who have been chicken soup for our souls!

Jack's family: Inga, Travis, Riley, Christopher, Oran, and Kyle for all their love and support.

Mark's family: Patty, Elisabeth, and Melanie Hansen, for once again sharing and lovingly supporting us in creating yet another book.

Dahlynn and Ken's family: Lahre, Shawn, and Jason, for their love and patience. Another book is completed and now it's time to celebrate!

Our publisher, Peter Vegso, for his vision and commitment to bringing Chicken Soup for the Soul to the world.

Patty Aubery and Russ Kamalski, for being there on every step of the journey, with love, laughter, and endless creativity.

Barbara Lomonaco, for nourishing us with truly wonderful stories and cartoons.

D'ette Corona and her die-hard dedication in helping to create quality books time and time again. Her ability to work with myriad coauthors and titles at the same time is wondrous and speaks volumes about her dedication to the Chicken Soup brand and name.

Patty Hansen, for her thorough and competent handling of the legal and licensing aspects of the Chicken Soup for the Soul books. You are magnificent at the challenge!

Veronica Romero, Teresa Collett, Robin Yerian, Jesse Ianniello, Lauren Edelstein, Lisa Williams, Laurie Hartman, Patti Clement, Meagan Romanello, Noelle Champagne, Jody Emme, Debbie Lefever, Michelle Adams, Dee Dee Romanello, Shanna Vieyra, and Gina Romanello, who support Jack's and Mark's businesses with skill and love.

Michele Matrisciani, Carol Rosenberg, Andrea Gold, Allison Janse, and Katheline St. Fort, our editors at Health Communications, Inc., for their devotion to excellence.

Terry Burke, Tom Sand, Lori Golden, Kelly Johnson Maragni, Patricia McConnell, Kim Weiss, and Paola Fernandez-Rana, the marketing, sales, and public relations departments at Health Communications, Inc., for doing such an incredible job supporting our books.

Tom Sand, Claude Choquette, and Luc Jutras, who manage year after year to get our books translated into thirty-six languages around the world.

The art department at Health Communications, Inc., for their talent, creativity, and unrelenting patience in producing book covers and inside designs that capture the essence of Chicken Soup: Larissa Hise Henoch, Lawna Patterson Oldfield, Andrea Perrine Brower, Lisa Camp, Anthony Clausi, and Dawn Grove.

Doreen Hess and the customer-support center and shipping department at Health Communications, Inc. Without you, the place would come to a grinding halt!

Shayla Seay for keeping our office running smoothly, taking care of all the small matters so we can concentrate on the big picture. Your loyalty, professionalism, and effervescent smile and laughter speak volumes about your dedication to this project. Thank you!

Our glorious panel of readers who helped us make the

final selections and made invaluable suggestions on how to improve the book:

Shana Avalos, Catherine Barczyk, Michele Caprario, Denise Carr, Bill Falkenstein, Colleen Gannon, Angela Hall, Sue Ann Hemphill, Julie Kaufman, Gail Kulhavy, C. J. Johnson, Scharre Johnson, Renee King, Debbie Marks, Del Marks, Jennifer Martin, Cindi McKowen, Kathleen Partak, Joyce Rapier, Sallie Rodman, Donna Rogers, Shayla Seay, Zacch Seay, Diane Smith, Joanne Thompson, Teresa Tjaden, Aileen Van Noland, Hanna Van Noland, Jeanie Winstrom, and Deb Zika.

To everyone who submitted a story, we deeply appreciate your letting us into your lives and sharing your experiences with us. For those whose stories were not chosen for publication, we hope the stories you are about to enjoy convey what was in your heart and in some way also tell your story.

Because of the size of this project, we may have left out the names of some people who contributed along the way. If so, we are sorry, but please know that we really do appreciate you very much.

We are truly grateful and love you all!

Introduction

We wrote *Chicken Soup for the Soul Celebrating Brothers &
Sisters* by virtue of the experiences gained from growing
up with our own assortments of siblings. Numbering a
total of fifteen amazing and wonderful souls amongst the
four of us (if you don't believe us, just read the dedication!), the relationships we have formed with our sisters
and brothers define who we are today.

Over the past several months, we have had the pleasure
of reading hundreds upon hundreds of stories submitted
for consideration. We found that the thread that runs
through each of these stories follows the same thread that
binds families. For most of us, that thread is more akin to
a heavy rope woven to form a net, a net that holds our
families together closely and securely, yet allows each of
us the freedom to swim out on our own—to experience
life, love, failure, and success. The safety of our "sibling
net" seldom drifts too far away, remaining open for our
return should life come crashing down around ourselves
or our sisters and brothers.

We also have learned that throughout our lives, it is
our sisters and brothers who generally are the most
accepting and understanding of our needs and who can
best provide us with just the right amount of support—

or head-knocking reality. And we are only too happy to return the favor! After all, with few exceptions, our siblings are likely the only people in our lives who we will have known from our births to our graves.

Reading these stories brought back so many memories of our relationships with our own brothers and sisters and reminded us of how blessed we are to have our siblings. We know you will experience the same when you read this book. And when you finish, please share it with your sisters and/or brothers. They, too, will realize the blessings in their lives—namely, you!

Share with Us

We would like to invite you to send us stories you would like to see published in future editions of *Chicken Soup for the Soul*.

We would also love to hear your reactions to the stories in this book. Please let us know what your favorite stories are and how they affected you.

Please submit your stories on our website:

www.chickensoup.com

Chicken Soup for the Soul
P.O. Box 30880
Santa Barbara, CA 93130
fax: 805-563-2945

We hope you enjoy reading this book as much as we enjoyed compiling, editing, and writing it.

1

CRAZY KIDS

Happiness comes only when we push our brains and hearts to the farthest reaches of which we are capable.

Leo Rosten

Priceless

The auctioneer pointed at my brother and said, "Sold!" Paul was the proud new owner of a 1989 collector's edition teddy bear, still sealed in its original box. Paul's eyes flashed with dollar signs when he picked up his newly purchased item.

Paul has always been interested in antiques, and even though this fluffy white bear wasn't an antique yet, he anticipated that it would definitely be worth holding onto. The see-through box that preserved the "priceless" creature appeared to be in perfect condition. Because the seal had never been broken, as Paul very well knew, the value of the innocent-looking stuffed animal was significantly boosted.

That was three years ago. Even then, at the tender age of twenty-four, I had not yet outgrown my passion for cute, cuddly, stuffed animals. And this bear was no exception. To Paul, it was merely an investment. To me, however, the plush white fur, the velvet red dress, and the black button nose all seemed to cry out for only one thing—love! I was holding the box on my lap for the long drive home when I suggested, "Let's open the box."

Shock and disbelief almost made my older brother run

the car off the road. "Are you crazy?" he asked. I knew that money and greed were his motives for keeping the box closed forever. But the more he resisted, the more adamant I became about wanting to release that stuffed bear from her lifelong imprisonment.

Our "Battle of the Bear" had begun. For the next few years, each time I visited his home, that 1989 collector's edition teddy bear was modestly displayed for all guests to "ooh" and "aah" over. I remained firm in my beliefs that no stuffed animal should be denied the ultimate embrace of human love. We were at an impasse because according to my stubborn brother, that bear would never take one breath of fresh air. Its value came from the fact that it was sealed in its original box. I had no chance of ever changing his mind.

Then hard times fell upon my brother. An unfortunate financial catastrophe surfaced at an inopportune time of year—Christmas. We had always exchanged expensive, lavish gifts. That particular year, however, he sadly explained he would not be able to afford our usual gift exchange. But Christmas is more about giving than receiving, so I went ahead as usual with my holiday shopping, expecting nothing in return.

Christmas morning arrived. We gathered at our parents' house to exchange presents. It was a happy time, and I delighted in giving gifts to my family. When all the presents were finally unwrapped, Paul disappeared for a moment and then returned with a big, beautifully wrapped box. Paul handed the gift to me, mumbling that it wasn't much. In disbelief that he got me anything at all, I tore open the gift: it was his collector's edition teddy bear, still encased in its clear box. He said, "Now you can do with it what you please."

For some people, greed over receiving a valuable collector's item might have intervened in the moment that followed, but for me there was never any doubt. I ripped off the lid to the box and, for the first time, let this stuffed animal bask in fresh air and human love. To most, this "collector's item" is now worth nothing. But to me, my beloved stuffed bear will remain forever priceless.

Sandra Toney

Snake Attack

The only thing we have to fear is fear itself.

Franklin D. Roosevelt

There was just a bit over one year between my brother Tommy and me. We seemed to be cut from the very same cloth—small, blond, shy, and mischievous. We did everything together and loved each other deeply. When I think back now, it was almost like we were twins, except for the seventeen months between us.

There were two older sisters and two younger brothers besides us, and we were all pretty close, but my Tommy and I had a deep bond. That closeness didn't last long, though, when we would get into trouble! He always hightailed it to a good hiding spot when we were discovered sticking our noses in where they should not have been.

Once we were playing in our backyard where there were several huge holes that had been dug for some poles. Our parents gave us strict orders not to go near them. I remember Dad telling us that there were snakes in the holes and that we would be in real trouble if one of us fell in. Well, I fell in! We were chasing each other around the holes during a game of tag. I tripped and down I went, tumbling into a dry, dusty, and loose-earthed pit. The wind was knocked right out of me as I landed on my back. Fine clouds of dirt rose into my brother's face as he lay flat on his belly, calling out my name. I gingerly sat up, wondering what had happened. I was hoping that the ground underneath me would not cave in and swallow me up.

"Glady! Glady! Are you okay? Oh boy, you're in big trouble. You're not supposed ta' be down there!"

"Whad'ya mean, I'm not supposed to be down here! You pushed me in! Go get Mom." *Ohhh! I was going to pound him a good one when I got out of there!* I promised myself.

It seemed forever before Tommy returned. I began looking around my dirt-wall prison and wondered at the plants and roots that grew into twisted embraces. I heard a small movement behind me, and I turned to see if it was that bratty brother of mine tossing in little rocks just to scare me into thinking that it was . . .

"Snakes! It's snakes! They're coming to get me! Mommy! Mommy! Help! I'm gonna die! Mommy!"

I began to claw my way up the rounded sides of the pit, pulling on any plant or branch I could see. I would get close to the top and then slip back down again. I didn't dare look behind me because I was certain there must have been at least forty snakes by this time, all slithering around each other, just waiting for me to fall into their evil circle. I kept clawing and as I kicked up more dirt, the opening of my dirt tomb became a tornado of dust rising in a funnel-like fashion.

Suddenly, I could feel something touch my back and then a heavy yank pulled me upward. I screamed and fought and kicked all the way up! I was so panicked by the sight of the six-foot-tall boa constrictor that had me in its clutches, that it took a good loud yell in my face to realize it was my dad. He had lifted me from the hole and tried to hold on to me, but my skinny knees were pedaling an invisible bicycle in a desperate run for my life. Once I was calm, I was scolded and sent to the house.

I couldn't understand why I didn't get a spanking for going into the hole and why my parents were laughing after I left. Once I got to the bathroom, I looked in the mirror and let out a shriek! As I was trying to get out of the pit, the loose dirt and dust came down onto my face, into my mouth and hair. My clothes were covered in dirt and all you could see were the whites of my eyes, my nostril holes, and two crooked lines streaking down each cheek from "fear tears." My teeth were blackened with mud and my hair stood straight up in sections with unseen dirt bows.

No wonder they couldn't punish me—they were laughing too hard at the sight of the punishment I had put myself through. My little brother Tommy laughed the loudest. I know he took his sweet time calling our parents because it was probably a payback for something I had done to him. Tom is gone now, but my memories of my brother live as lovingly today as they did yesterday.

Glady Martin

Zip-a-Dee-Doo-Dah

In simplest terms, a leader is one who knows where he wants to go, and gets up, and goes.

John Erskine

My brother Blair was three years older, and I believed he could do anything. So I wasn't particularly surprised when he knocked on my bedroom door one day and announced that we were going to build a zip line. Even though I wasn't 100 percent sure what a zip line was, I figured he did, and I was thrilled to be included in his adventure. But I soon figured out why he felt compelled to include his little sister.

"We'll use your bedroom window," Blair said.

"Why not yours?" I wondered aloud.

Blair explained that his window, on the side of the house, was too close to the neighbor's tree. A line stretched from his window to the tree would be too steep. My window, at the far corner of the front side of the house, was the perfect starting point. "Besides, your window is right above the porch so we can stand on the porch roof when we climb out your window." It sounded like Blair had thought of everything.

Years of Boy Scout training came in handy as Blair expertly tied one end of a long rope to the corner of my bed. Next, I watched with fascination as he threaded the rope through a pulley block and threw the free end out the window.

Our father had died four years earlier, when I was five and Blair was eight, and I was amazed at all the handy things my brother had somehow taught himself. I had plenty of book smarts, but less of the mechanical skills and initiative I admired in him.

Blair tied a second rope to the pulley. "This is how we'll pull it back. Hold this." He ran downstairs.

From my window I watched Blair tie the free end of the rope around the sturdy trunk of our neighbor's pine tree. He leaned and pulled and pulled until the rope was tight.

"Everything alright up there?" our babysitter called from the kitchen. Mom was away and had hired the sitter to keep an eye on us.

"We're fine," I called back, oblivious to the fact that my definition of "fine" and her definition probably differed significantly.

Back upstairs, Blair examined his knots one more time. "Let's try it!" He shoved the pulley, and we both cheered as it whizzed down the rope. Pulling together, we hoisted the pulley back to my window ledge and Blair tied a loop in the rope below the pulley block.

"Wanna send Harry next?" I asked, thinking that sending my stuffed dog down first would be a good test.

Blair straddled the ledge. "Nah, you hold the end of the rope for me." And before I had time to protest, he was gone.

Then I learned why this setup is called a zip line. The empty pulley had moved gently down the rope, but this time Blair's weight made the pulley zip wildly toward the tree. I screwed up my face, anticipating impact, but Blair had the sense to let go of the rope, tumbling to the ground a few feet before the pine tree, so he didn't smack into it full speed.

"Whoo-oo!" he pumped his fist in the air. "That's great!"

I dragged the pulley up and Blair ran inside and leaped out the window again. This time, however, he lowered his feet as he reached the yew hedge at the side of our property and dragged his feet through the hedge to slow down.

After several flights, Blair took the end of the pulley rope from me. "Your turn," he said. "Hang straight down and you'll slow up fine."

"Me?" I fancied myself as his assistant, not a full partner-in-crime. When I peered out the window, the ground looked a mile away. "I'm not sure."

"Don't you wanna?"

I thought for a minute and said, "I do, but . . ."

"You can do it," Blair said without hesitation.

And I believed him. I eased through the window, grabbed the loop, and stepped off the edge. And he was right—it was great!

In hindsight, Blair was sorry he had told me to try it. I didn't fall or get hurt or anything like that, but my shrill scream of joy was so loud that the babysitter came running. Blair briefly convinced her that our mother had never said we couldn't do this, and the babysitter let us skim down the rope a few more times before she came to her senses and banned our fun. It was over all too quickly.

I think the babysitter would have preferred not to mention the whole episode, but when Mom came home, we had to come clean—the impromptu use of the yew hedge as a braking system had permanently disfigured several bushes. My mother looks back on this episode as the day her crazy kids were lucky not to kill themselves. I look back, smiling, remembering the day my big brother taught me to fly.

Wendy Greenley

Got Raisins?

I'm the youngest of five children, and we grew up in a very rural area of the Adirondacks near the tiny town of Pottersville, New York. We all had old bicycles most of the time, and occasionally they needed repair. By age ten or so, I was pretty good at it.

One particular morning, I went to get my favorite cereal, Raisin Bran, from its ceramic container. To my great confusion, I didn't see any raisins. Not one. Just flakes. I emptied the whole thing. No raisins. I started to think that my parents had bought a defective box with no raisins in it and had poured it into the container without noticing.

Then I saw it—a piece of paper at the bottom. Still not suspecting foul play, I unfolded it and read: *I have asked you for days to fix my bike. If you ever want to see your raisins again, you will fix it today. —Diane*

Blackmailed by my sister! What a crummy (not to mention time-consuming) trick to pull! But it worked. I fixed her bike right away. The raisins, having been held hostage in a sandwich bag without even any air holes, were returned.

Now Diane is forty-six and I'm forty-four. I think I'll give her a call and tell her I'm over it.

Glen A. Carlsen

Terrified Together

Laughter is the shortest distance between two people.

Victor Borge

My brother Jerry and I sat in the backyard and bemoaned our state of poverty. We were two broke teenagers with no jobs in a tiny Texas town. How were we going to survive the summer?

"Let's take out an ad."

"Yeah, we'll do any job."

"No job too large or small."

Jerry and I scraped our change together and placed an ad in the local paper.

"No job too large, too small?" mumbled a low, tired voice on the phone a few days later. "Pick ya up at 7:00 AM."

The next morning, a horn blared from the driveway of our home. After bursting through the front door, we came face-to-face with a heavy man in stained black overalls. He was standing beside an old model pickup filled with odds and ends of work materials. A large dog was inside the cab of the pickup.

"Hop in the back of the truck," the man said by way of introduction. "Time's a wasting!"

We bounced and jostled down some secondary roads and then turned off on a sandy back trail barely large enough for the truck. The road wound through swampland and patches of pine groves. Finally, we pulled into a clearing.

"Get busy," the man snorted. He pointed at a pile of red bricks with cement plastered on them. "Knock the cement off these here bricks so they're good again."

The old man handed Jerry and me each a hammer and then walked to his little trailer under a shade tree. Hours passed and it seemed like we had hardly done any bricks at all when the old man returned.

"Lunch," he barked. "In the trailer!"

By this time, the two of us were getting a little edgy. I followed my brother into the trailer. Surprisingly, it was cool and dark. After looking for long sharp knives, coils of rope, and duct tape, and finding none, I sat down in a folding chair. Jerry sat beside me. The boss grabbed the largest cast-iron skillet I had ever seen and plopped it on a stove burner. Then he flung open a door next to the stove. I flinched, expecting the dead bodies of the last workers who'd been desperate enough to come and knock cement off of bricks. Stunned, I stared at rows and rows of shiny unlabeled cans. *Home-canned victims?* I worried to myself.

"Every meal is a surprise," the old man said, with a smile I could detect through his straggly gray beard. "Unlabeled cans are cheap. Good deal."

I sure hoped that he had bought the cans at some discount place. I looked at Jerry and he looked at me. *Perhaps there was hope for us yet,* I thought.

After opening several cans, he dumped the contents into the heated skillet. Then he poured dark, thick molasses on top. We ate in silence. The sticky sweet substance was not recognized by my taste buds, but neither of us dared to make a comment.

"Time for music," our boss decided after he collected our plates. "You play the guitar?"

We both shook our heads in the negative, but a job was a job. The old man placed guitars in our laps and then taught us a chord.

"Play the chord when I say," he yelled over the strumming of his own guitar. For the next little while we strummed our newly learned chord. Finally, when the noon sun turned to afternoon shadows, we headed back outside.

"Bit cooler now," the old man said as he pointed to several rows of plants. "Weed the garden."

For the rest of the afternoon and into the evening, my brother and I pulled weeds. *Digging our own graves? Not! Weeds grew only so deep, not enough for burial.*

"When are we going home?" Jerry whispered as the late afternoon turned to dark. It was almost impossible to see the difference between weeds and plants, and we were getting more nervous.

"It's time," the old man's gravelly voice broke through the darkness. *Time? For what? Surely, not the END! Were we ready? Could I save my brother? Could I save myself?* Before I had a chance to raise my garden hoe in defense, the old man commanded us to get into the truck.

"Time to take you kids home," he said as he waved us out of his little garden patch. My brother and I scampered into the back of the old pickup. Maybe the guy was not a creature of terror. Maybe we *were* going home.

Clinging to the sides of the pickup bed, Jerry and I swayed with the ruts in the road. Soon we were home. I wanted to throw myself on the ground and kiss the soil like some kind of disaster or war survivor, but instead, I jumped down and stood by my brother. The old man climbed out of his truck. He slowly reached into his front overall pocket without saying a word. *Heaven help us,* my thoughts screamed

The old man pulled a thick, black wallet from his pocket. He took out a wad of money and peeled off enough bills to cover the one-dollar-and-seventy-five-cents-an-hour wage for each of us.

And then he left, just as he came. When he was gone, Jerry and I just looked at each other, and then we started laughing. We laughed at the fact that we were alive and home, in one piece. And we had even been paid for being terrified, together.

Renee Hixson

Payback

*E*verything *happens to everybody sooner or later*
if there is time enough.

George Bernard Shaw

My fortieth birthday was rapidly approaching, but it could not have come at a more inconvenient time in my life. By the time I was forty, I was supposed to have the hot red sports car, time to travel, and the money to finance all my outings. Instead, my husband and I were suddenly starting over. The company for which he had worked for almost twenty years was closing its local facility, and we were faced with a bleak, uncertain future.

Because it appeared that I would have to be the primary breadwinner, I was back in college with cohorts far younger than me, seeking an advanced degree to increase my income potential while searching for a higher paying job. My husband had also decided to go back to college and constantly scanned the want ads in the hopes of finding a new career. Between school costs, our monthly budget, and preparation for the unknown, finances were tight. There most definitely was not a sports car in the immediate future, nor would I be traveling to any exotic locales.

As my birthday drew nearer, I made it very clear to my family, as well as to my brother and sister, that I did not want any hoopla. Instead, I wanted the day to pass quietly and uneventfully. I did not want any reminders of what "should have been" on my fortieth birthday.

While my husband, children, and mother respected my wishes, I should have known my brother and sister would not let an opportunity like my fortieth pass without incident. How naïve of me to believe that my siblings would not secretly plan something to commemorate the event! My brother, sister, and I are close in age and have always searched for excuses to plot and plan. We grew up in a neighborhood with few children our age, so it was just the three of us. Together, we built forts and tree houses in the woods and even constructed impenetrable dams across the creek behind our house. And after reading the Foxfire books that were popular in the 1970s, we decided to build our own moonshine still, despite the fact that we had no idea what moonshine was.

As we grew older we continued to plot and plan, though the ulterior motives differed from those of our younger years. We doubled- and occasionally triple-dated, and every once in a while, we covered for each other when explaining to our parents the reason for breaking curfews. We kept secrets among ourselves. I promised my brother never to mention the little incident that occurred while leaving school one day a little too rapidly, and my siblings and I agreed not to bring up that little run-in at the lake with friends. Ours was a trio that was one for all and all for one.

Of course, there were times, fortieth birthdays for instance, when the plotting and planning involved two of the three of us at the expense of the one left out. My sister was the first to turn forty, so my brother and I secretly stole to her house in the dark of night and planted forty pink plastic flamingos adorned with Christmas lights in her front yard to remind her and all her neighbors of her special day. How could the two of them not reciprocate on my big day?

The first clue I had that something was up was the ringing of the telephone very early on the morning of my fortieth birthday. At first, I thought that my body was betraying me. Here I was, barely forty, and I was already hearing a ringing noise in my head! When I finally realized that it was the phone and not my aging ears, I answered and heard the familiar voice of an old business associate on the other end wishing me a happy birthday. Groggily, I listened and thanked him for his well wishes, but then it occurred to me that he had never called me on my birthday before. In fact, how did he know that I was turning forty?

"Well, sugar," he drawled, "I saw the sign out on the highway!"

I sat up in the bed, now wide awake. *What in the world was he talking about?* I thought. I quickly hung up and yelled for my husband and children. They bounded in the room, full of smiles and good cheer. I demanded to know what they had done. All three swore that they had not participated in any sign-making endeavors. Their surprised faces convinced me that they were indeed innocent. Then, the telephone rang again. I picked it up and was greeted by my little brother's loud guffaw.

"Hey old lady!" he shouted. "So, you were able to hobble to the phone, huh?"

And that is when I knew who the culprits were—my brother and sister! I demanded to know where this sign was advertising to the world that I was now officially a middle-aged woman. This simply brought another round of laughter from my dear, sweet brother.

"You might want to take a drive down the road, old lady," he said. "There's a whole lot more than one sign out there on the street!"

I quickly hung up the phone, grabbed my car keys, and raced out of the house in my housecoat and slippers. Despite my forty years, if I moved quickly enough I thought I could muster some damage control. That is when I got my first glance at my car. Written all over it in vibrant colors were birthday messages. My name and age were visible for all to see. Knowing that the early morning light would hamper the ability of passers-by to decipher the messages on the car, I jumped in the front seat and raced down the driveway. There, at the end of the driveway, was yet another fortieth birthday announcement! However, the poster-sized sign mounted on the mailbox for my neighbor's viewing pleasure was not as bad as I expected. It would just have to wait. I was more concerned with the larger public display. I sped through the neighborhood, and there it was at the entrance to the subdivision facing the main road—a huge banner on display for all to see!

I did not know whether to laugh or cry. *So much for dismissing my fortieth birthday!* Whether I wanted to ignore it or not, my brother and sister had made certain that I would be acknowledged. As the sun slowly rose in the morning sky, I came to my senses enough to realize that it would not be appropriate for a middle-aged woman to attempt to get the sign down while in her nightgown. That would certainly be a more embarrassing public display. I could not help but smile at my brother and sister's antics. *Maybe forty won't be as bad as I thought.*

When I walked back in the house, the telephone was once again ringing. This time, it was my sister, who was a bit kinder in her greeting. After all, she had already reached that forty-year milestone. Together, we laughed at the display, and, as she reminded me, I had it coming after the little flamingo incident. Before hanging up, I assured her that the sign at the entrance to the neighborhood would be coming down very quickly.

"Sign?" she asked innocently. "Don't you mean signs? Um, you might want to drive a little farther down the road."

All day long, I received birthday wishes from friends, neighbors, acquaintances, and even the mailman who had seen the two massive banners proclaiming, "Lordy, lordy, Terri Duncan is forty!" I also learned that my brother was the mastermind and financier behind the fortieth birthday signage plan, but I have forgiven his trespasses. After all, he turns forty this year. My sister and I have been plotting and planning for months!

Terri Duncan

I Scream for Ice Cream!

I'm the oldest of five. There are three of us in a row, girl-boy-girl, each one a year apart, then two years later, another brother, and four years after him, our youngest sister. Although great friends today, we had the usual squabbles growing up.

My being the oldest—and a girl—was hard for my brother Larry because he wanted to be in charge. Especially hard was the fact that I was so good and did everything right in my parents' eyes. While I will admit (now) that I just never got caught, he did.

When I was a teen, our family moved into a bigger house and we each had our own room. Mine was in the finished attic and included a separate half-bath. Larry's was in the basement, converted from the former family/ play room, and included the previous owner's bar (which we never used) and a large freezer behind the bar. Outside his room were the washer/dryer and storage shelves for extra canned goods.

Every Sunday, our mother would make her famous rib roast dinner. During the week, we drank only milk with our meals and never, ever, ate dessert. But Sunday was the lone, eagerly anticipated exception to the dessert rule.

One Sunday, my father sat proudly at the head of the table and complimented my mother. "Great meal, Pat! I think we should finish it with something special." Like a king, he summoned my brother: "Larry, go downstairs and get the Breyer's." Feeling extra generous, he added, "And bring up some Hawaiian Punch, too."

Larry didn't move. *Why wasn't he jumping up and running downstairs?* I wondered. While we kids sat antsy at the table, he remained motionless in his chair, looking down at his empty dinner plate. Back then, in the 1970s, Breyer's was the premium ice cream—and, though hard to believe, the *only* premium ice cream—and Breyer's Chocolate Chip Mint was the family favorite. When it went on sale, my mother would buy one, sometimes two half-gallons, storing them in the large freezer in the basement for just such a special occasion. Hawaiian Punch, usually reserved for birthday parties, was a real treat, too, since we rarely drank soda or sugary drinks.

But what was wrong with Larry? He appeared as if he hadn't even heard our father announce this double surprise. "C'mon, Larry, go downstairs and get it!" our dad urged.

Slowly, Larry pulled back his chair and shuffled down to the basement. *How puzzling. He was an ice cream lover like Dad. Why wasn't he rushing?* As slowly as he left, he returned, placing the half-gallon carton on a plate in front of Dad. Mom passed bowls and spoons to him so he could serve the family.

I remember seeing Larry hang his head even lower, staring intently down at his feet. He looked absolutely nauseous. *Oh well,* I thought as the rest of us eagerly watched Dad open the flaps at one end of the carton and push the ice cream scoop—right through! Astonished, he quickly opened the other end. Three quarters of the carton was empty!

"I don't believe this! Breyer's sold us an almost-empty carton of ice cream!" Dad shouted as he held up the light-weight carton as proof for all of us to see. There was only about two inches of ice cream left in the container. It didn't even cross his mind that there might be another reason. Ha! Not me. I wasn't fooled. Peering laserlike at my brother, I suddenly realized he wasn't sick. That face was the picture of guilt!

Sitting across from my brother, to the right of our father, I stared directly at Larry and sweetly asked, "Larry, can you think of any other reason why the ice cream disappeared?" Eyebrows around the table rose as everyone quickly understood my implication.

"What are you talking about?" he rebutted, acting innocent. Dad was a lawyer and took control. An honest and fair man, Dad was well known for his patience, too, but not when you messed with his ice cream.

Larry broke down. He confessed that his ice cream sneaking began with just a few spoonfuls. Then he did it again, then again, a few more spoonfuls, then a few more, all the time eating neatly from the same side until he had eaten almost straight through, like a prisoner digging his way out of his cell.

Our parents were angry! Together, they yelled at Larry. We four kids joined in the chorus. Larry's face reddened. His eyes swelled. Although physically a strong teen, and not one to show his emotions, he was near tears.

Suddenly, Dad stopped and sat back. Everyone grew quiet. During the long, audible sound of silence, I wondered what was going to happen next. It couldn't be good. *Larry was really going to get it this time!* Then Dad started laughing; no, he started howling.

"Why are you laughing, Al?" Mom said, still angry.

"Think about it, Pat. We're upset because our kid, a fifteen-year old teenager, ate ice cream when other parents are worried about their kids doing drugs." Mom smiled and then started laughing, too.

I couldn't believe it! Instead of being livid, they were relieved! Now it was my turn to be enraged. *Do I have to do drugs in order to get some ice cream and Hawaiian Punch around here?* Still smiling, Mom went into the kitchen and came back with an opened bag of packaged cookies. Sullenly, we ate them. Looking across the table at Larry, I saw him smile. My brother had gotten away with it.

Kathy Shiels Tully

Reprinted by permission of Off the Mark and Mark Parisi. ©2007 Mark Parisi.

Super Strong

*Even if you are on the right track, you'll get run
over if you just sit there.*

Will Rogers

In a two-story house close to the Gulf of Mexico, in the
quaint little suburb of Seminole, Florida, two brothers and
one sister wrestled while they waited for the hard, humid
Florida rain to pass by. They leapt from couch to couch,
pouncing on one another while imitating their favorite
wrestler. Sweat formed on their foreheads, breaths began
to last longer and start deeper. This wrestling match was
getting really intense, then suddenly someone called for a
"super strong" break.

I know what you're thinking: what's a "super strong"
break? I'm glad you asked. "Super strong" is the original
Red Bull. Developed in the 1980s by a boy (my brother)
who wore tie-dye shorts, high-top tennis shoes, and a
bright holographic shirt, this drink allowed immunity
and ultimate strength to whoever was brave enough to
consume the unknown liquid concoction.

I remember it like it was yesterday. I'd sit there waiting for my brothers to announce our day's adventure. As much as I hated being locked up in the house due to Florida's typical afternoon showers, I secretly waited for the days we wrestled. So many people assumed wrestling was just for boys. But it was also cool to be a girl who wrestled, especially when I made a quick move and faked out my opponent—a.k.a. my older brother.

Besides the calorie burning, wrestling was a bonding experience. My brothers were always a little more gentle with me, and at an early age I learned the power that a woman has over men. I learned how to bat my eyes and put on a puppy-dog face to manipulate a situation. But that's beside the point. I also learned that when you let your brother make up a drink with whatever he can get his hands on from the kitchen, the obvious outcome is a drink that is anything but soothing. That must have been why we called it "super strong."

If you're confused, let me explain. During a wrestling match, if you felt weak, or if you were getting beat, you simply yelled, "suuuuuppper strong!" and you ran to the brother-made drink sitting on the counter just waiting for the brave soul who was desperate enough to gulp it down in ten seconds or less. Once the very brave wrestler finished the drink, he or she was able to do what they wanted for thirty seconds, and no one could touch him or her. This led to a pretty interesting wrestling match.

Often, not long after the "super strong" was downed, the match came to an end. Around that time, the usual thirty-minute rains were slowly making their way back into the gulf, and children's voices began to flood the streets once again. We would quickly join them, and my brothers would find the rest of the guys and start doing their guy things. I would find my girlfriends and immediately turn back into a "lady," impressed with the cute boys playing tag in my front yard, and my Barbie dolls.

I don't remember telling my friends about our "super strong." I figured they wouldn't get it. I assumed they would have no idea just how cool it was to be my brothers' sister. On the outside, it looked like we hardly played; we had to keep it cool in front of others. We all knew how "uncool" it was to admit you liked your siblings. But we also all knew the truth. No matter how much of a show we put on for others, we couldn't fool ourselves.

I never knew what other families did while they were stuck inside during the rains. I never asked. I never worried about it. I knew that no matter how cool, how fun, and how rich those other families in the neighborhood were, none of them was drinking "super strong."

Today we are adults, with adult lives. Yet, when the world seems so much more than I can handle, I long for the rainy days that imprisoned my brothers and me in our imaginations—those days when a glass of "super strong" could make any one of us able to conquer all that was in our way. Little did we know that the day we created the game, we were also creating long-lasting memories of fun, bonding, and the ability to hope. We were teaching ourselves that all it takes is a little faith and confidence to beat our opponent.

Even though we no longer play the silly games of yesterday, I still have my siblings, and I still have them on my team, "super strong" or not.

Michelle L. McCormick

2

WE ARE FAMILY

*The only rock I know that stays steady,
the only institution I know that works,
is the family.*

Lee Iacocca

Circle of Eight
and Strawberry Shortcake

*The happiest moments of my life have been the
few which I have passed at home in the bosom of
my family.*

Thomas Jefferson

I called all seven of my siblings so they'd help pass the
word to other family members about our annual reunion.

This year our reunion would be bittersweet—the last
time all eight siblings would be together. We were the
"Circle of Eight": five girls and three boys, all middle-aged
now. But we would not be the Circle of Eight for long: our
brother was dying of cancer.

M.P., as everyone called him, had fought hard, enduring
intense chemotherapy. But the cancer had spread to his
spine, causing paralysis. There would be no more treat-
ments. Confined to a wheelchair and weaker each day, his
outings were few. Yet his will and spirit were strong.
Forming our special circle one last time was important to
him.

As I planned ︙ bered the conversation M.P. an sked, "Sis, do
you have M pe?"
"No, I su lowed a recipe.
She carrie I know she used
Bisquick
"No crust recipe made
from slice it, and slather
butte e on crushed sweet
stra

gone by she did, but in
la enience generation. She
as used for lots of things,

s twinkling. "You're busting
ver she did, her shortcake was
rest of the girls to see if one of

, I was back at M.P.'s home. He
e lack of a shortcake recipe.
"I ut of five sisters not one of you got
her recipe, ied.

I wished I ha. at recipe. *Anything to make M.P. happy,* I
thought. Then I had an idea. I started to plan.

With the reunion just days away, I phoned my sisters,
explaining the dilemma. "Pull out your aprons. We're having a Strawberry Shortcake Taste-Off. I challenge each of
you to make your version of Mama's strawberry shortcake. Our brothers will judge, with M.P. having final say.
What do you think?"

My sisters thought it would be a hoot and were confident they'd have the winning shortcake. So was I. The
game was on.

Reunion day arrived, and while the rest of the family
was outside eating, visiting, and playing games, we sisters

slipped away. My husband soon followed. We crowded into the kitchen, spreading ingredients on the table and across the counters.

"No cheating," my husband yelled, aiming the video camera, zooming in on each of us. We giggled and carried on like children, trying our best to be secretive and furtive as we prepared strawberries and mixed, stirred, and rolled dough.

Bakery aromas wafted through the kitchen as we removed our masterpieces from the ovens. We combined our individual strawberry mixtures with our shortcakes. We had five perfect shortcakes, each a little different, made by five sisters, each expecting to win. We scooped our concoctions into identical bowls, covered them with clear wrap, and taped our names and numbers to the bottom. I was the fourth sister so I taped "#4" on mine. We shuffled the five dishes, and then we each grabbed a bowl. Having no idea whose recipe we carried, we lined up, ready for the taste-off.

My husband hurried outside, camera in hand, and announced to the crowd, "We've got a surprise for you! M.P. recently brought it to his sisters' attention how disappointed he was that none had their mother's strawberry shortcake recipe. So today, the girls have a little friendly competition going. They've been cooking up their version of the mysterious shortcake. And now, let's hear it for the Strawberry Shortcake Sisters and the first ever Strawberry Shortcake Taste-Off! Music please!"

The *Rocky* theme blasted through the air as my sisters and I, in birth order, danced, strutted, swayed, and laughed our way across the deck toward our brothers. We held our bowls high in the air with one hand and jabbed and punched the air with the other. We did Rocky Balboa proud. The crowd clapped and cheered.

The look on M.P.'s face was priceless. Our other two

brothers stood wide-eyed. Their smiles spread from ear to ear as they slapped hands together and hooted in admiration. We girls hammed it up until the music hit the final note.

"Okay, M.P.," I said. "You wanted Mama's strawberry shortcake. Now it's up to you and our brothers to sample these fabulous creations and choose one that tastes most like Mom's."

M.P. rubbed his hands together. "No problem. I'll know it when I taste it. I've got that flavor imprinted up here," he said, pointing to his head. M.P. was intense as he removed the wrap and took a bite from each bowl. Next, the other two brothers sampled the cake and whispered back and forth.

"This one's out. I taste cinnamon. Ma never used cinnamon," M.P. said.

"This one can go too," said the two others. A third bowl was quickly discarded. The three of them had narrowed the choice to two. M.P. took a bite from each remaining bowl. The others did, too. Each took several more bites, serious in their judging. The brothers held a hushed conference and the crowd watched eagerly in anticipation.

M.P. held up a dish like it was a trophy. "We have a winner. This one tastes most like Ma's. This next one is close. We give it second."

Someone hollered, "Tell us who won!" My sisters and I joined hands and held our breaths.

M.P. removed the name from the bowl, grinned, and said, "Drum roll, please. The winner is: "Sis #1, our oldest sister! Second place goes to Sis #4. Hmm, says here her secret is Bisquick! Not bad—for second."

Everyone cheered, yelling congratulations, celebrating our strawberry shortcake taste-off as if it was as important as a Rocky win. Sis #1 and I smacked high fives and whooped and strutted a little more as we made

a final victory lap. My other three sisters laughed and demanded a retaste! Everyone else lined up for shortcake.

M.P. said, "Since my job was so tough, I'm saving some
of the winning shortcake for later. Big sis, you'd better
document this recipe. Give all your sisters a copy. Strawberry shortcake is a tradition for this bunch."

Three weeks later, we lost M.P.

Now when we gather for our reunion, we pull out the
video to get a glimpse of M.P. and the Circle of Eight playing, laughing, loving—and being a family. In honor of M.P.,
we make sure to have plenty of "Mama's strawberry
shortcake" on hand. We all use the winning recipe from
"Sis #1" when we make it now.

Each of us savors our sweet memories, and though we
are seven now, we will forever be the "Circle of Eight."

Linda Cook

Mom separates the black sheep from the scapegoats.

Gimmies and Do-Overs

The secret to playing Ping-Pong with my brother, Kevin, lies in his eyes. If there's a twinkle in his eyes, I know there's also a devious smile on his face, and he's planning to serve straight down the outside line.

His serve is low and fast. He often adds a spin to the ball, and if I return it too high, he's likely to slam it right back at me. But if I catch the twinkle a split second before he swings his paddle, I move a half step to the left and slant my paddle just enough to return the ball to his weaker left side. We're both right-handed, and we know each other's strengths and weaknesses.

When we were growing up, our games were all about winning. We attacked each other's weaknesses as much as we concentrated on our individual strengths. Like typical teenagers, we argued about the score, slammed paddles on the table in anger, and stomped out of the room when we lost. There's a half-inch chunk missing from the table in Mom's basement, and we're both positive the other was responsible for it. When our parents joined us for a game of doubles, we fought to have Mom as our partner. She moved out of the way faster than Dad, even though we knew Dad's serves were stronger.

When we left home for college, then for careers, Mom packed the net and paddles in a plastic bag and turned the table into a storage area for books and home decorating magazines. She added photos, scrapbooks, and other memorabilia she inherited as relatives passed away. There were no Ping-Pong games for nearly fifteen years because Kevin and I were too busy with jobs, spouses, and babies.

Then, one winter, Mom decided that her grandchildren needed the table for Ping-Pong more than she needed it for piles of paper. She sorted through her table of memories and dreams, dusted off the paddles, and bought a new net. Once again, her basement rec room came alive with pings, pongs, and outbursts that alternated between frustration, anger, and laughter.

My kids (ages fifteen, twelve, and ten) are now avid players, and we spend hours in Mom's basement when we visit. During the Christmas holidays, when both Kevin and I are visiting with our families, the games have evolved into a double-elimination tournament. In each of the tournaments, Kevin and I have met in the finals, though the kids play more competitively each year.

"This isn't a gimme anymore, is it?" he conceded after a game with my twelve-year-old, Geoff, during our 2006 tournament. Kevin would now have to fight his way to the championship through the losers' bracket.

"You didn't let him win, did you?" I asked.

"No, I just missed—a lot. He's really gotten good." His tone of voice and saucer-shaped eyes told me he was a little surprised, a little embarrassed, and very humbled. Then Kevin raised his voice as Geoff walked by: "You earned it fair and square, Geoff. Good job, but I'll be ready for you next time."

The games that followed were punctuated with laughter, competitive spirit, and light-hearted banter.

"How long have you been practicing that?" Kevin teased, when his nephew's shot grazed the table's edge and dropped straight to the ground. In another game, when his niece's serve missed the table—for the third time—he suggested a redo and turned a frustrating situation into a compliment: "Your serve's getting a lot better. That one was really close."

I listened from upstairs, thankful that the brother who hurries downstairs to choose the "better" side when I'm his opponent is also the uncle who believes that games with his niece and nephews include an unlimited number of do-overs.

I first noticed Kevin's "uncle-ness" fifteen years ago, when he held our firstborn. He gently cradled Nathan and marveled at his strong grip; he did the same when Geoffrey and Ellen were born. As they've grown, he's done what many aunts and uncles do: given them noisy toys for their birthdays, swam with them in the wave pool, and treated them to ice cream before dinner. But there's something different about how Kevin does it.

The result is *Real*—with a capital R—and much like the "Real" in Margery Williams' classic story of the velveteen rabbit. When someone really loves you, the toy learns, you become Real and it lasts forever.

And that's probably why my kids simply refer to my brother as "Uncle" and see no need to further define who he is by adding "Kevin" to the title.

Back at the Ping-Pong table, I noticed that my kids' eyes don't twinkle like Kevin's; they still look directly at the spot they're serving to. But my oldest shouldered up to me after one of his last games and said, "Uncle showed me how to put a spin on my serve. You better watch out!"

I will. But this year, I reigned: 15 to 12.

Karna Converse

Tickets to Our Future

Parents are the bones on which children sharpen their teeth.

Peter Ustinov

The travel bug bit my parents at a young age, and when my little brother, Jeff, and I came into this world, they wanted to share the bug with us, too.

When we were younger, we had great fun as a family exploring the United States via long road trips. But our parents really wanted to take us on a plane . . . to Europe! They had made many trips before and after they were married. My mother was a flight attendant for National Airlines so travel was affordable—and they loved it. For years, Jeff and I heard stories about their trip, and we so badly wanted to go to Europe. However, for a now stay-at-home mother and a middle-management father, a trip to Europe for four did not fit into the family's everyday budget.

So, we saved for the "big trip." Every frequent-flier mile Dad earned went toward our airline tickets, and Mom squirreled away grocery money. When Dad had accrued enough miles for four airline tickets, my parents began planning our European trip: seven countries in four weeks. They purchased our Eurail passes and secured our passports, and then we were off on the trip of a lifetime. Little did they know that this trip would be a family bonding experience that would determine the direction of their now-teenage children's lives.

Dad was responsible for carrying "the purse," our family's travel bag. A combination backpack/fanny pack, the purse held the water bottle, money, maps, passports, and the new family bible—*Europe on $30 a Day*.

Jeff and I were allowed to bring only one small bag that we had to be able to carry for long distances. I couldn't bring a hairdryer or curling iron, which was devastating to a fifteen-year-old girl. (I still cringe at the photos of the air-dried hairstyles I wore throughout the trip!) But we two kids wised up to the luggage rule and would sneak our personal things into "the purse" so Dad would unknowingly be stuck carrying our stuff!

Since our parents were running the show, Jeff and I were content to sit on a bench and read or hang out while they converted money, telephoned the hostel or pensione where we were staying, figured out the maps, subway systems, or buses, and struggled with the different languages while asking for directions. We didn't do much to assist, except complain when things didn't work out. Mom washed our socks and underwear in the sinks of the tiny rooms we rented and hung them out to dry overnight before the next day's adventures.

Eight years after our memorable trip, my brother and I, now ages twenty-two and twenty-three, traveled together again. This time we traveled throughout Eastern Europe. When we'd hop off a train at each city and set about finding our way around, we'd laugh together and reminisce about our first European adventure with Mom and Dad. We talked about how unappreciative we were of our parents then: It's so much easier to travel when someone else does the work for you! We were now responsible for carrying "the purse" (which had morphed into a backpack by then), deciphering the bus schedules, converting foreign currency, and washing our socks and underwear at night in a tiny sink.

Today my brother and I are thirty-seven and thirty-eight, respectively, and we are forever grateful to our parents for the years of sacrifice they endured just to take us to Europe. The travel bug has bitten us both; together or apart, I have been to over thirty countries and Jeff to over sixty. Because of our love for travel, I have shared the world with my husband and three children. Jeff works abroad for the State Department as a Foreign Service officer, having dedicated his life to helping make the world a better and safer place. But we both still recall that first trip to Europe with the fondest memories. It opened our eyes to possibilities and bonded our hearts to each other.

Kellie Randle

Wishful Dreams

I knew it was a shot in the dark, but I had to tell someone my deepest desire: I wanted my brother to acknowledge me on my birthday. I spoke cautiously to my husband about my wish.

Looking at me as if I had just asked him for a miracle, he replied, "You know, sweetheart, I don't think I would count on it."

"Oh, it doesn't matter anyway," I muttered.

Knowing I was adopted, I had searched for my biological family and discovered I had a brother, twenty months younger than me. Before contacting my brother, I imagined how he might react to having part of his hidden past revealed. I thought we would bond naturally because of our shared beginnings. When I got the courage to write him, I didn't anticipate his answer would be one of silence. Although I respected his feelings, there was still a part of me that wanted to know him.

My birthday came and went, and my brother didn't acknowledge me.

I was, however, thrilled with my husband's present: a chartered fishing trip on the Pacific Ocean. Fishing was my ultimate pastime, but my husband and I don't share a mutual love for fishing. I would be going on this trip solo.

On the day of my birthday fishing trip, I had butterflies in my stomach. I found a seat toward the back of the boat as it got ready to leave the dock. Over the sputtering engine, I heard a man chatting with a couple about Idaho.

I was born in Idaho, and for several years, I had been searching for answers about my adoption from that particular area, a place far from where I now live. I jumped at the chance to ask if any of them were from Idaho.

The friendly man said, "Yes, I'm from Hailey, Idaho."

I'm sure the look on my face would have been worth a million dollars. Hailey is where my long-lost brother lived. Hesitantly, I told him my brother's name. I was shocked when he said, "I know your brother; I work with him." I felt as though I had just found a tunnel leading to part of a buried treasure.

My new boating friend was not sure why he had decided to embark impulsively on this fishing trip. The only other time he had been on a swaying boat on the ocean, he vowed it would be his last. For the next five hours we took turns talking each other out of becoming seasick. Neither one of us believed it was just a coincidence that our paths crossed that day.

And so, there we were, strangers huddled on the tumultuous waves of the ocean, speaking with God together. He told me as much about my brother as he knew, describing him as a warm and compassionate human being. He promised that when the time was right, he would talk to my brother about our fishing adventure.

One Thanksgiving, long after that fateful fishing trip, a letter arrived. My brother's sincere words spoke to my heart. Learning that the two of us were separated by adoption came as a shock to him. After all this time, my revelation had stirred up the past, leaving no easy fix.

We wrote letters to each other for almost a year, with no promises or expectations for the future. Getting acquainted was like traveling down a blind alley. By sharing his thoughts with me, my brother had become the sensitive and caring person my boating friend had described. Just as I was starting to feel like we weren't total strangers anymore, he abruptly stopped writing me for no apparent reason. I felt a tremendous loss. I wrote him several times asking him for an explanation, but his silence continued to hurt me. A part of me wanted to travel the 600 miles to talk with him face-to-face, but I couldn't beg him to love me as his sister. I had to let him go, again.

This year on my birthday, I once more shared with God my long-standing prayer. I whispered, "You know I still believe in the impossible. Please, I want to hear from my brother." I wiped away my tears before anyone would notice. Deep in my heart, I felt God had let me down.

When the florist delivered a beautiful flower arrangement for my birthday, I tried to guess which friend might have sent them before opening the card. As I read the words, "Love, your little brother," I looked around the room expecting to see God standing there. Breathless, I felt like this little girl who had reclaimed her lost baby brother. I sobbed as his thoughtfulness soothed my hopeful heart.

I know it isn't going to be a happily-ever-after story for us, but I believe my brother and I will have a relationship nurtured by time and patience. No matter how long it takes.

JoAnne Bennett

The Final Touch

When you look at your life, the greatest happinesses are family happinesses.

Dr. Joyce Brothers

"What childhood memories do you treasure?" I asked my three children, now all young adults.

"Every Easter you made a carrot cake in the shape of a bunny," answered Lori. "I liked the black jelly beans for eyes and the uncooked spaghetti for whiskers."

"I remember at bedtime you would say, 'The first one in bed gets the very first kiss,' and we'd race to dive under the covers," said Betsy.

"I hate to admit it, but I think our crazy competition with the Eiffel Tower was awesome," said Steven. All three nodded in agreement.

The Eiffel Tower competition began innocently enough one summer while our family was camping in France. After a day of sightseeing in Paris, we trudged across the grass as we left the Eiffel Tower. Suddenly, twelve-year-old Betsy sprinted from under the famous landmark.

"Guess what?" she said. "I am the person in the family

who touched the Eiffel Tower last!"

Six-year-old Steven burst into tears. "That's not fair, Bets!" he sobbed. Betsy responded with a victorious grin. We didn't visit Paris again together, but over the years the three younger family members eventually made their way back.

When Betsy and Lori were in high school, they mowed lawns and babysat to earn enough money to revisit Europe. They made an effort to visit Paris so they could touch the Eiffel Tower together.

Another summer, Lori lived with family friends in the Netherlands. When they spent a week in Paris, Lori became the one who last touched the tower.

While Steven was in college, he and a friend backpacked around Europe. After he returned I asked him the important question: "Did you touch the Eiffel Tower?"

"Of course I did!" he replied without hesitation. "Now *I'm* the one who touched it last!"

After Lori's wedding, she and her husband traveled to Europe. When they talked about their honeymoon, she made no mention of touching the Eiffel Tower. Then she showed the family her photo album. The page of honor was reserved for three important pictures. The first focused on Lori's hand in the foreground with the Eiffel Tower in the background. She labeled it, "Will she?"

The next picture captured Lori's hand inches from the Tower. The caption read, "Getting closer!"

The last picture showed Lori's hand on the Eiffel Tower. The words read, "Yeah! She did it!"

The competitive siblings have since lost track of who touched the Eiffel Tower last. It's no longer important. What is important is making precious family memories, whether it's an Easter bunny cake, a bedtime kiss, or a silly sibling competition like being the last one to touch the Eiffel Tower.

Miriam Hill

The Batter and the Box

"Mommy!" Karl said, running from the dugout, his arms full of gear. "Look what the coach gave us."

I took the pint-sized blue and gold jersey, held it in the breeze, and read the back: *Buck Henry's B&G*. "Your sponsor's the bar and grill?" I glanced around a sleeve and eyed my nine-year-old shortstop.

He grinned. "Now all your friends can root for our team," he said. I visualized betting pools and scoreboards with little squares and shuddered.

"Guess what else we got?" Socks, sweatshirt, and a medium-sized supporter tumbled to the ground. He shuffled through the pile, suddenly popping up like a fly ball, holding a package under my nose. "Candy!"

"Fund-raiser chocolate bars?" I read the item count: *twenty-four bars per box at one dollar each.*

"For the team," he said. He peeled open a box, snatched a long one, and ripped back the wrapper. "And the person who sells the most gets a ten-pound candy bar."

I snagged a second liability from his hand. "How many boxes do you have?"

"Five!" His eyes sparkled. I gulped and did the math in my head: *One hundred and twenty—minus one.* "We can come back for more. Coach has plenty."

"I bet he does." I waved to the enthusiastic coach and begrudgingly hauled away boxes, begging to define the "fun" in fund-raiser.

On the ride home, I tapped my fingers on the steering wheel and strategized as boxes of calories weighed down the back seat. *Maybe I could sell them at work?* Nah, established territory reigned during peak season. Key spots for selling fund-raiser products were already overwhelmed by coworkers with seniority. I was a newbie.

Grandma and Grandpa? No, the hundred-mile ride pushed the profit margin to the negative column. I racked my brain for creative disbursement.

"I have an idea." I turned into our driveway and said, "You and your sister can stand outside Buck Henry's and sell candy." *After all,* I thought, *Buck is a co-conspirator; he might as well get into the game.*

"Cool, I'll tell Erin." Karl scooted out of the car, arms overloaded with Little League dreams. I hustled behind, eager for a quick sale.

Inside, I dug through drawers. I tossed the kids bright yellow shorts and plastic helmets with a yellow A's sticker.

"Why do we need to wear these?" Erin peeked out from the oversized helmet.

Karl pulled the trunks away from his skinny legs and frowned. "I look like a lemon."

"Marketing," I said. A final search netted a pennant flag featuring an elephant lifting its trunk and tooting, "Go A's."

"I'm not holding that thing." Karl backed away, palms planted high in protest.

I sensed a player strike. "Erin?"

"No way!" Her golden curls bounced in negative agreement. She stood alongside her brother: two against one.

I conceded the battle and rallied on. "Got your money box? Candy?" We headed out to put our plan in motion.

Outside the tavern, Karl held the candy box while Erin cradled the money container. I sat in the car and waited to signal the kids when a potential customer approached.

Then . . . a customer! I made eye contact with Karl. We locked stares. I tapped my chest, stroked my fingers down my arm, and tipped my nose. He pulled his right ear lobe. Message received. The customer is at the plate. I watched and waited. *What? No purchase? Probably a low-carb guy.*

A couple stopped and the woman spoke to Karl. My son stood soldier-stiff. Erin huddled by her older brother, quiet for a first-grade chatterbox. Stalemate. With a shared glance, the twosome walked away, empty of calories.

A patron exited the grill. "What're you selling?"

Karl's mouth dropped open as he shuffled on his feet, but no words of sale escaped. With a shrug, the man sauntered away. Three up, three out. I called the kids to the car window. "What's wrong?"

The freckles on Karl's face outshone the fear in his pale blues. "You said never to talk to strangers." Trapped by a technicality, I slumped in the seat. *There has to be a fundraiser clause in the parenting handbook.*

"Get in the car. I have an idea."

"Not another idea," Erin whispered, reconsidering her duty to her brother.

After a quick trip to the store for marking pens and construction paper, we were back at our spot with an added prop—a little slugger bat posed over Karl's right shoulder. Good touch.

Brother and sister on the same game plan, ready to go for the win.

"Aren't they adorable? What's in the box?" A crowd gathered. Bases loaded.

On cue, Erin flashed a large sign. *Candy bars, one dollar each.* A woman opened her purse and Washington crossed home plate.

"Where's the money going?" Buck's cook jingled four quarters in his palm.

Karl flipped a second piece of bright construction paper. Purple crooked letters answered: *Support Little League Baseball.* Karl's face lighted with the sale. He pulled out a third sign: *Thank you.*

Coins and dollars dropped into the box, chocolate bars exited right and left. Not a word was spoken in the night air to a stranger. Score one for Mom.

At evening's end, I flung the last empty container into the garbage bin, pulled three candy bars from my pocket, and said to my winning brother and sister team, "It's all in how you play the game that makes you a winner." Then I gave them each a victory candy bar, and kept one for myself.

Cynthia Borris

New Adventures

A journey of a thousand miles begins with a single step.

Lao-tzu

I exhaled slowly as I straightened my shoulders and lifted my head. I forced a smile as I contemplated my future.

"I can do this," I reassured myself under my breath. Inside I was not so sure.

It was the day after Christmas 1994. As a recent college graduate, I had decided to put my degree in international relations to practice by spending the next year in war-torn Angola, in southern Africa.

My family accompanied me to the boarding gate (in the days before heightened security and fears of terrorism). Moments before the final boarding call, I savored my last words with each of my family members, as well as our farewell embraces.

Mom hugged me first. I was the baby of her four children. She beamed with pride as she held my hands. Not only was she proud of my courage in taking on this important work to help a country and a people in a critical time of reconciliation, but she also could see herself in me. Thirty-six years earlier, Mom made a similar voyage to Angola to instruct Angolan teachers in the art of teaching. But that was before the war of independence and the brutal civil war that devastated the country and its people. I was cognizant of the fact that the country I was about to encounter was markedly different from the country that my mother had experienced many years earlier. I could not guess how right I was.

Daddy followed Mommy and gave me a bear hug, as well as a rushed list of instructions: "Take lots of pictures, write in your journal daily, and send lots of letters."

"Yes, yes," I agreed as I patted him lovingly on the back.

Crystal-Lion, my eldest sister, was next, squeezing me in her warm hug and promising to pray for me. I knew she would, and that knowledge comforted me.

My only niece, four-year-old Bunny, squeezed me in her tiny arms and declared her love for me. I would miss my little one, and I planted big kisses on her chubby cheeks to prove it.

My brother-in-law (or my second brother) put his hand on my shoulder and warmly looked me in the eyes. "Enjoy and be safe, my sister," he said. I hugged him and promised to do both.

Carolie, my second sister, was next. She squealed my name: "Bevie! I'm going to miss you. Be strong, girl. I love you."

I smiled as I return her excited embrace. I would miss my semi-twin—especially since we had been living together for the past several months.

My brother, in his characteristically nonsentimental fashion, began rushing me along. "C'mon Bev, time to go. No crying. Just enjoy yourself and be safe." He gave me a big hug.

My mom rushed to give me a final hug. There was such love from my family that I suddenly became unsure why I was leaving. The thought made my bottom lip quiver. I promised myself I would remain strong as I boarded the plane. Turning around to wave at my clan, I saw each of them waving, smiling, throwing me kisses, and cheering me on.

"We love you, Bevie!" I heard their combined cheer. I smiled in appreciation, as tears threatened to spill over. With one last look, and a huge smile to mask my fear, I rounded the corner of the passageway to the plane. I would miss them.

As I took my seat and collected myself, my airplane neighbor remarked to me, "You sure do have a supportive family."

I smiled and nodded in agreement. My reverie was interrupted by a commotion near the entryway. I saw my brother emerge from around the corner. He scanned the seats until he spotted me.

"Bev, if you need anything, *anything,* just call me, okay?" His nonchalant demeanor was replaced with real concern, as if he had just recognized where his baby sister was headed. "Be good, be smart, and have fun." He pushed some money into my hands and gave me one last hug.

That time I couldn't stop the tears. I didn't even try.

Beverly Watson

"Sissy always gets the front seat!"

Best Buds

"Hurry up, Kari! We've got to get to our fort before they kill us!"

My brother Jared and I ran as fast as we could, out of breath, trying to reach the safety of our fort. We raced to the tree and started climbing. He reached the inside of our makeshift fort, leaned down, and stretched his hand out to help me up the last few steps to safety.

This was a typical day in our lives. We were always playing make-believe games—cowboys and Indians, cops and robbers, or whatever else he saw fit to play at the time, which I always went along with. Jared was my hero. Out of my four brothers, he and I were the closest in age and spirit, and we always got along splendidly. Though he was nineteen months older, people always thought he was younger than me because he was shorter. I remember going to Shoney's and the server would bring him a little red child's cup and I would get the adult glass. That never failed to irritate my big brother.

As I grew up, Jared was my protector, my comrade, and my best friend. He never let anyone talk down to me, and he would often take punishment for my wrongs just so I wouldn't get in trouble. He told me things that he would never dare tell another soul. He treated me just like he treated all his guy buddies. One time when I was nine, he dared me to walk across an ant-infested, fallen tree. After accomplishing my oh-so-heroic feat, he said, "Wow, Kari, you did something a boy would do!" Those were high words of praise coming from my brother.

He kept every secret I ever told him. Whenever I needed anyone to talk to, I went to him, and vice versa. But the older Jared grew, the wilder and more free-spirited he became, and we grew farther apart. Oh, we still talked and had fun together, but he grew just a little bit more distant.

The day Jared told our parents that he was joining the Marines was the day I really learned how to fake what I was feeling for my brother, the brother who knew me better than I knew myself. I was shocked, proud, and terrified. My mom was a basket case. He would be her second son to join the military. My dad was strangely quiet about it all. They were supportive of his decision, but they did not want him to go. I wanted to scream at him, vehemently protest his decision, but I did not. I could not, for I knew that I was the only one who could sway him from doing what he was born to do. I was not about to put him in that position. He finally came around to asking me what I thought about his decision, so I lied.

"Whatever floats your boat," I said, barely able get those four little words out of my mouth. My eyes filled with tears, but I brushed them away. I would not stand in the way of his dream.

The dreaded day came for him to leave for boot camp. I could not say good-bye. *Nothing will ever be the same again,* I thought. There would be no more secret discussions. He would never again come into my room at night, waking me up by prodding me with his deer antlers because he wanted to talk. He would no longer be there if I needed him, and I would not be around if he needed me.

The Jared that left for Marine boot camp that day was not the same Jared who returned twelve weeks later. The new Jared stood straighter, exuding confidence and maturity. And of course, as with all Marines, he was oozing with cockiness. He was different. Things had changed, plain and simple. We were unable to talk much in the months following his graduation from boot camp. He went on with his training, and I went on with my normal daily activities, missing our old camaraderie.

Last May, our entire family took a month-long vacation to Georgia. To our excitement, Jared was able to join us for a weekend. After picking him up from the airport, our family spent all day together at the lake near our cabin. On the ride back from the lake, everyone was drained from the sun. Jared and I were in the backseat, both wiped out. I leaned my head on his shoulder, asking him if he minded.

"No, it's all right," he replied.

"What are brothers for if not for their sisters to lean on, right?" I asked.

He was quiet after my playful comment. I looked up a few seconds later to see tears rolling down his cheeks. I quickly looked down, but I was shocked. My immovable, unshakeable, rough, tough Marine brother was crying, crying because of the statement that I had made. That's when I realized that even if we no longer played cowboys and Indians, or built sloppy forts, that I was still important to my brother, even if he tried not to show it. From then on, I knew that no matter how old or how far apart we might be, I would not only be my brother's little sister, but I would always be his best friend.

Kari Mills

No Joke

We must accept finite disappointment, but never lose infinite hope.

Martin Luther King Jr.

Slowly, quietly, and painstakingly, I gently wrapped one shoelace around the other. The trick was to make a good sturdy knot that created exactly the right distance between his sneakers. *So far, so good,* I thought. My brother Todd had not even twitched in slumber. A giggle almost escaped my lips as I pictured the upcoming moment. I carefully positioned myself well out of his trip zone, but still able to have a great view.

Okay, one, two, three . . . "Fire! Fire!" I screamed at the top of my lungs. Pickles, my brother's pup, joined me in my sudden declaration by ripping into a barking frenzy.

Then it happened. Todd sat straight up and threw his wiry legs off the bed. With his next move he stood up to run away from my imaginary fire and fell flat on his face.

I roared hysterically as he glared at me, until I noticed that he just about had the knot undone. Realizing bodily harm was imminent, I ran for my life.

It was like that when we were kids. This and a hundred other incidents defined our relationship. We were three years apart, but that didn't stop the practical jokes we played on each other. It might sound a bit strange, but it was our own form of *kid speak* that said, "I love you, even if you are yucky."

Shortly after the tripping incident, when we were four-teen and seventeen, our mother died of multiple sclerosis. The practical jokes instantly subsided as we chose to cling to each other in grief. Being the older sibling, I assumed the responsibilities of "motherhood" as best I could. From that point forward, the playful sister left and the caregiver was born.

My brother developed a relationship with a new best canine friend, who often eased his pain better than I could. Pickles was part Basenji, part who-knew-what, but the mutt was a furry little genius. The dog was absolutely filled with love and a willingness to do anything my brother asked. Pickles knew when to play and when to nuzzle. She would try anything in the way of tricks that Todd could dream up, far exceeding the standard "sit up," "play dead," and "roll over" doggy routines. The two were inseparable. I once saw her floating down a creek while standing upright and balancing on an inner tube tied behind my brother's tube. Nothing could keep her from his side.

Years later, after I was married and had a family of my own, Todd always assumed my dinner invitations included Pickles. Then one summer, my brother asked a favor that I lived to regret. "Hey Sis, can you keep the mutt while I go on vacation?"

I didn't hesitate. "Sure, bring her over."

I hadn't lived with that dog for a while and had forgot-ten how friendly and easygoing she could be. On the first morning she was in my care, I got up and opened the front door for her to go outside. I had no fear of her running away. Pickles had always known her boundaries and who her family members were.

A car drove by slowly, and initially I thought nothing of it. Then, to my surprise, it stopped and the door opened. I looked up, expecting to give directions to a neighbor's house, but instead, the passenger whistled and Pickles jumped in. I stood on my front porch, clutching my bathrobe in shock, as my brother's most prized treasure sped away.

Todd had only been gone two days when he called to check on Pickles.

"How's the mutt?"

"She's been kidnapped," I whispered, dread filling my being and tears filling my eyes.

"Nice one, Sis," he laughed.

No, no. He thinks I'm teasing him. Why did this have to happen while I had her?

"Todd, I'm so sorry. I'm not playing." I told him the story.

The hollow sound of his voice reverberated in my heart as he spoke. "There was nothing you could've done. She's just a dog. Don't worry about it, Sis." His need to comfort me was not half-hearted, but his sorrow seeped through.

I tried my best not to feel guilty about Pickles. My brother tried even harder to convince me that he held me blameless. Slowly, over the next couple of months, with his continual assurance, I forgave myself.

A few months had passed when one morning I heard scratching at the door. Since it was 5:30 AM, I thought I was dreaming at first, but the persistent scratching pulled me out of bed. I stumbled through the kitchen and peeked outside. I couldn't believe my eyes. No worse for her absence and acting as if it were three months earlier, Pickles was patiently pawing the back door and wagging her tail!

My hands were trembling as I dialed Todd's number. I held the dog in my lap, afraid, for some silly reason, to let her go.

"Todd? Are you up?"

"Yeah. Is something wrong, Sis?" His voice was filled with concern.

"No, something is right," I cried—literally. "She's here, Todd. She just appeared at the back door."

"Who's there?" I'm sure he thought I'd lost my mind.

"Pickles is here. Come get your mutt before she takes another ride," I laughed.

We will never know where she was or how far she had to travel to get back. But there is no doubt in my mind that her love for her best friend kept her looking constantly for a moment when she could make her escape and return.

Nowadays we again playfully tease one another in a grown-up way. But neither of us will ever forget the time a big sister wasn't joking.

Melanie Stiles

3

STORIES SHARED BY YOUNGER SIBLINGS

Wisdom begins in wonder.

Socrates

The Snow Moon

Children love to be alone because alone is where they know themselves, and where they dream.

Roger Rosenblatt

A friend of mine was reminiscing about when she and her sisters were little. They used to spend long summer days in their garden playing in the gazebo. She was brought up in Virginia and moved to Scotland, where I live, once she married.

My childhood memories are so different. My brother, Harry, and I were brought up in a small terraced house on a lane. We had a garden the size of a postage stamp, and the nearest thing we had to a gazebo was our dad's smelly old shed.

There was only a year between Harry and me. I don't know if it was the closeness of our ages or the fact that money was short and we had to pull together, but my brother and I were very close. We shared everything—not just food and treats, but more important, secrets and dreams.

The memories that my friend from Virginia brought back to me were of Harry and me on snowy winter nights. We shared a bedroom in those days, when we were about ten or so, and we would press our noses to the window and watch the snow falling. We both loved snow, and Harry could always tell when it was coming. He would look up to the sky and say, "That's a 'snow moon.' It's on its way!" More often than not, he was right.

One night when we couldn't sleep, we put on all the warm woolly clothes we could find, took the cover off Harry's bed, and went out silently to Dad's shed. It had been snowing heavily and Harry's snow moon shone its silvery glow everywhere. We knew Dad never locked his old shed and we went inside, sat down on an old box, and wrapped Harry's bedcover around us. We had on boots, gloves, and woolly hats, and really, we were quite warm, even with the shed door open.

It wasn't snowing and there was no wind; everything was silent and beautiful. "There is no moon like the snow moon!" Harry declared. "It makes the snow shine like diamonds, doesn't it?"

We sat there and Harry began to tell me about how he wanted to be a famous artist, painting magical scenes that people would put up in their homes. "Everyone will want to have one of my paintings, because they will be so different," he said.

We talked about his magical paintings and my dreams of being a famous pianist, wowing audiences worldwide— until the snow moon disappeared behind some gathering clouds.

"Time to go inside," Harry said. "It looks like there could be more bad weather coming." We gathered up Harry's bedcover and stepped out into the night, closing the shed door.

We returned to the house and tiptoed back up to our room, unaware that two sets of footprints led to the shed and back. Fortunately for us, the snow came down so heavily that night that it covered up the evidence for us.

Harry and I remained close, and when he was about to go to art college, he received a scholarship offer in Australia. My older cousin and her husband lived there and Harry went off to live with them while he studied. I missed him terribly and wrote to him all the time. When mum got the call that Harry had been in an accident and hadn't survived, she didn't know how to begin to tell me.

I was seventeen and it broke my heart never to see my beloved brother again. We couldn't afford to go to Australia for Harry's funeral, and my cousin and her husband paid for Harry's body to come back and be buried at home in Scotland.

Three years later, when I was twenty, I went to spend a holiday with my cousin and her family who lived near Perth in Western Australia. We spoke about Harry and the year he had spent living with them. "He missed you so much. He talked about you all the time," she told me. "I have kept something for you. I didn't want to risk sending it to you."

She took me into one of their spare rooms and there, hanging on the wall, was a picture of our back garden in the middle of winter. Snow was sparkling everywhere in the moonlight, and there was a little boy and girl wrapped in a bedcover, huddled together, smiling, and looking out into the night. "He called it the *Snow Moon*," she told me. I burst into tears.

I am fifty-eight now, and Harry's painting still has pride-of-place in my living room. I see him as large as life every time I look at it and know the bond between us will never break.

Joyce Stark

A Hero in Her Eyes

One afternoon when I was picking up my two children from school, my daughter's fourth-grade teacher motioned me aside.

"I have to tell you a story," she said in a whisper. "Today I asked the children to name their favorite athletes. One boy raised his hand and said, 'Michael Jordan.' Another said, 'Magic Johnson.' All the children were naming famous athletes. Then I noticed Christy's hand go up."

The teacher smiled at me and asked, "Who do you think Christy named as her favorite athlete?"

"I have no idea," I said.

"Her brother! That's what she said: 'My brother is my favorite athlete.'"

Christy's teacher gave me a quick hug. "Isn't that the sweetest thing you've ever heard? I had to share it with you."

I thanked the teacher for telling me the story and walked to the car with Christy. A few minutes later, her sixth-grade brother, Jim, jumped into the back seat. I had no idea how this little girl could idolize her big brother—the one who seemed to torment her day and night. Rarely did I see a tender moment between them. Then I remembered the awe I felt for my two older brothers when I was growing up. In my eyes, they could do no wrong.

Like most big brothers, my son could be a real jerk to his little sister. But in her eyes, he was her hero. And now that they are both grown, he is still her hero—and her favorite athlete. Just ask her.

Jeanne Pallos

Long Live the Queen!

You don't choose your family. They are God's gift to you, as you are to them.

Desmond Tutu

I have always looked up to my sister. *Always.* You see, back when we were teenagers, I would lift her petite frame to the top of the refrigerator where I would keep her, much like an angry queen on a very uncomfortable throne. Some may call it teasing, but I prefer to think of it as a creative way to show my love and admiration for her. After all, I thought women liked being put on a pedestal.

My sister Ann was born on December 13, and I arrived in this world the following December 4. Despite our close ages (and supposedly same gene pool), we couldn't have been more different. That is why I still want to have DNA tests done to confirm that we are in fact from the same parents.

From an early age I could see a tremendous difference between us. Ann, for one thing, was a good child, a smart child who was able to easily grasp things like reading and writing—things that evaded me for far too long. (What she lacked in spankings and poor grades I made up for in every painful sense.)

I never saw her study, so how could she make a 4.0-plus average without cracking a book? Some things come easy for some people. My parent-teacher meetings were like a broken record: "Tommy just needs to focus on his school-work" or "If Tommy were half as interested in his books as he was in girls, then he'd have straight As." Ann's parent-teacher meetings were short and sweet. "Ann can get into any university she chooses."

How could this happen? She got the beauty *and* the brains. Judging by my report cards, I was convinced that my teachers only knew two letters—D and F. It was *so* embarrassing to me that my age was higher than my ACT score while Ann's was about twice her age. Ann, as you might guess, was valedictorian or something like that. She gave a wonderful speech at graduation and seemed so comfortable speaking before the crowd. Some things come easy to some people.

Oh, and she could read music, too. Ann could sight read anything. I have always wondered how she could do that because I can't read a lick of music. (I ended my first piano lesson due to the "perfume" my male teacher wore that was not nearly masculine enough for my tastes.) To make matters worse, Ann played piano in church every Sunday. As I said, some things come easy to some people. She got pins for church attendance, while I got reprimands for being late to church, dressing inappropriately, or for miss-ing church altogether, forgetting that it was Sunday.

Next, Ann graduated from college with a nursing degree in only four years. I barely got my degree in just over eight years. And while I was still getting my undergraduate degree, Ann went back to get her master's degree in nurs-ing. Now, as a pediatric oncology nurse, Ann has spent decades of dedicated service to her patients and their families. As you can imagine, that particular field of medicine brings an added amount of stress to everyone facing such a tough adversary as cancer. Ann has done it with style and grace. Some things just come easy to some people.

I assume Ann learned her parenting skills from our mother, Lou, who has always been a great mother, because I have watched Ann as she mothered and nurtured her two children. They have grown to be wonderful young adults filled with talents and ambitions, due in large part to my sister's guidance and assistance. She has handled every difficult challenge in their lives by turning them into positive experiences—and making it look effortless.

From an early age, when she helped our father in his medical practice, Ann knew what she wanted to achieve in life. She has done those things. I, too, knew from an early age what I wanted out of life: to retire before ever going to work. So far I'm right on track. I've spent my life writing songs and loved every minute of it. I have had no greater fan and supporter than my sister Ann.

A brother could not ask for a better sister or friend. She has blessed my life and the lives of countless people. We are all better off for our time with Ann. She is kindness and goodness personified and neatly packaged in a petite frame. I have always looked up to her and still do, even though she is no longer screaming down at me from atop her refrigerated throne. Yes, I love my sister. Some things are easy for some people.

Tommy Polk

"Of course I'm behind you, sis—
I'm your biggest fan."

Ricky's Gift

I remember bringing my brother a sandwich. I sat on the kitchen floor and watched my mother make it—baloney and cheese on buttered white bread. I remember how tall Mom seemed and how thrilled I was when she said, "Can you take this out to Ricky?"

The sandwich was on a hard plastic turquoise plate. I stood up and Mom handed the plate to me. I remember holding the edges very carefully as I walked to the door that my mother held open. I remember how white the sandwich was on the green plate, with the baloney just peeking out from the edges of the bread. But I don't remember giving it to Ricky.

My brother died just before I turned two years old, but he gave me a gift that has turned out to be the foundation of my adult life—an education.

He grew up in times that were often hard, both mentally and financially. My parents were barely out of their teens when Ricky was born, and he was in his teens before they could afford a house, or even begin to think beyond living paycheck to paycheck.

It was different for me. I never knew Mom and Dad to worry about money. We weren't rich by any means. We didn't take expensive vacations, and my clothes and most of theirs came from Kmart or other discount stores. My parents bought bonds, however, and they always had substantial savings.

Mom told me it used to be different: "When your brother was little, I had to go to my grandma and borrow the money to feed him dinner."

My brother was nineteen years old when I was born. He was living at home, working as a mechanic to put himself through college. I often wonder what it must have felt like to him, suddenly having a baby sister, just as he was becoming an adult. My mother told me he moved out of the house just before I turned one year old, in part because it was hard to study around a crying baby.

After two years of community college, Ricky transferred to a local, four-year university. He was a business major. At about the same time, he took out a large life insurance policy.

It was 1969. Every kid his age must have been thinking about Vietnam and wondering if they could expect to have any kind of a future. But my brother had a student deferment, which at least ensured he could finish his undergraduate education.

Ricky died the last day of August 1970. He was at work filling a truck tire with air and the tire blew up. His death certificate says that he died almost instantly.

A few weeks before, he'd told our mother about the life insurance. He wanted her to know that it was for my education. Mom tried to talk him into canceling it. "You have so little money," she told him. "Don't make things harder on yourself."

But Ricky insisted. He said to our mother, "It's hard enough for me. It will be impossible for a girl to make any kind of a living without a good education by the time Lynn grows up."

That money allowed my parents to send me to an all-girls private school in the fourth grade, after I had been labeled a "slow reader" in the public schools. My experiences there laid the foundation for everything that followed.

At home, my parents said I didn't have to go to college if I didn't want to, and my father in particular wondered if it would be a waste of time for a girl and too expensive. At my school, however, going to college was expected and gender had nothing to do with achievement. When my acceptance letter for a great old liberal arts college three thousand miles from home arrived in the mail, I went to my mother first. I asked her if there really was no money for me to go to college.

She told me about Ricky's insurance policy. There was still enough left, as long as I took out some loans and received financial aid.

My brother, at the age of twenty-one, spent money that he didn't have to give a future to a sister he would never know. I can't imagine any love greater or more selfless than that. It's a gift that I will never forget.

Lynn Marshall

Three Little Words

To measure the man, measure his heart.

Malcolm Forbes

A few years ago, my older brother, Hector, became seriously ill and was hospitalized. News of his illness reached me by way of our sister, who said he looked bad. I called his hospital room, and after the third ring my brother answered.

"Hector, it's me, Leti. How are you?"

"Not good," he said point-blank. "I can't talk right now."

My heart went out to him in a split second.

"Yes, I realize that," I said. "I will call you later when you're feeling better."

"Okay."

"Take care of yourself," I told him. I should have hung up the phone. Every fiber of my being told me to, but I didn't. I stayed on the line and listened to the tormenting silence. Then, out of the blue, I blurted, "I love you!"

I waited for a response to my declaration of love, but after several moments of awkward silence, I said good-bye and hung up.

For the rest of the day, I wrestled with the same question repeatedly in my mind: *Why couldn't Hector say he loved me in return?* I was in the middle of dusting the furniture when it came to me. Through the years, Hector had indeed expressed his love for me—not through words, but through actions.

One particular example of that happened twenty-six summers ago. The end of another work-filled summer was just around the corner, and we Gómez kids were looking forward to getting back to school and giving our aching bodies a rest. We spent nearly the entire summer hoeing cotton and peanuts in southeastern New Mexico and the west Texas panhandle area.

Granted, destroying weeds under the piping hot sun is no dream job by anyone's standards, but for the underprivileged Gómez kids, it was the deal of the century. When the end of the hoeing season arrived, we had yet to buy our school clothes and supplies; we had squandered most of our earnings on unnecessary things. What can I say? But we had one last card to play. We were made an offer we simply couldn't refuse. Onion planting was about to begin and there was still time to make some dough for school clothes and supplies.

When we told our mother about this opportunity of a lifetime, she flatly refused to let us go. She was just as tired as we were.

"You children have never planted onions before. You have no idea what you're getting yourselves into," she warned us sternly. But we didn't listen. We were far too distracted by the green dollar signs in our big brown eyes. We begged and pleaded with her until we wore her down. So off to plant onions we went.

The first few days were grueling. Planting onions was not as easy as it sounded. In fact, it was kicking our butts. If you think I'm exaggerating, think again. Imagine having to waddle from side to side on your knees all day long, inserting tiny stalks of onions into the ground with your thumbs. We must have looked like the Munchkins from *The Wizard of Oz*, except, in our case, there was no yellow brick road to follow, only rows and rows of fertile soil. By the end of the day, our thumbs looked like chicken drumsticks. I have no idea how we were able to endure two weeks of this, but then again, back in those days we ate a lot of beans and tortillas. We were tougher than leather.

The night before our last day on the job, Mama came down with a wicked stomach virus and it was up to us kids to finish the job. *One more day and we could retire for the summer,* I thought. *We'd made it this far. Several hours more would be a piece of cake.*

Despite the threat of rain and a cold gusty wind blowing into our sunkissed faces, we began the morning strong. Little by little, we started to run out of gas, especially me. Even my brother J.R., the only one of us who could outlast the Energizer Bunny, was sucking wind. By midmorning we were ready to be hauled off the field on stretchers. But none of us would admit it; the only thing greater than the pain was our pride.

Ignoring our discomfort, we kept on working without saying a word, until I lost my balance and fell to the ground from exhaustion. Hector and J.R. abandoned their posts and hovered over me. I looked up into their eyes and said, "Help me up so I can go on."

My brothers each grabbed an arm and pulled me up. For a moment, Hector was at a loss for words. Finally, he broke his silence. "That's it for you. Go back to the truck. J.R. and I will finish your row."

I was torn. Part of me wanted to go back to the truck and slip under a warm blanket, but another part hated the thought of increasing their workload. I had two clear-cut choices: save myself or suffer right along with my brothers.

READER/CUSTOMER CARE SURVEY

We care about your opinions! Please take a moment to fill out our online Reader Survey at **http://survey.hcibooks.com**.
As a **"THANK YOU"** you will receive a **VALUABLE INSTANT COUPON** towards future book purchases
as well as a **SPECIAL GIFT** available only online! Or, you may mail this card back to us.

(PLEASE PRINT IN ALL CAPS)

First Name _____ MI. _____ Last Name _____

Address _____ City _____

State _____ Zip _____ Email _____

1. Gender
❑ Female ❑ Male

2. Age
❑ 8 or younger
❑ 9-12 ❑ 13-16
❑ 17-20 ❑ 21-30
❑ 31+

3. Did you receive this book as a gift?
❑ Yes ❑ No

4. Annual Household Income
❑ under $25,000
❑ $25,000 - $34,999
❑ $35,000 - $49,999
❑ $50,000 - $74,999
❑ over $75,000

5. What are the ages of the children living in your house?
❑ 0 - 14 ❑ 15+

6. Marital Status
❑ Single
❑ Married
❑ Divorced
❑ Widowed

7. How did you find out about the book?
(please choose one)
❑ Recommendation
❑ Store Display
❑ Online
❑ Catalog/Mailing
❑ Interview/Review

8. Where do you usually buy books?
(please choose one)
❑ Bookstore
❑ Online
❑ Book Club/Mail Order
❑ Price Club (Sam's Club, Costco's, etc.)
❑ Retail Store (Target, Wal-Mart, etc.)

9. What subject do you enjoy reading about the most?
(please choose one)
❑ Parenting/Family
❑ Relationships
❑ Recovery/Addictions
❑ Health/Nutrition
❑ Christianity
❑ Spirituality/Inspiration
❑ Business Self-help
❑ Women's Issues
❑ Sports

10. What attracts you most to a book?
(please choose one)
❑ Title
❑ Cover Design
❑ Author
❑ Content

TAPE IN MIDDLE; DO NOT STAPLE

FOLD HERE

Do you have your own Chicken Soup story
that you would like to send us?
Please submit at: **www.chickensoup.com**

Comments

After thinking it over, I handed Hector my burlap sack, which was half-filled with onions yet to be planted, and started my long journey to the truck. All the way back, I couldn't help but feel grateful that my older brother was letting me escape my misery. He knew I was dying inside. He also knew I'd never quit on my own accord. He loved me enough to let me save face. He loved me enough to relieve me of my duty in an honorable way.

I'm happy to say we all made it through the day in one piece. On the way home, Hector and J.R. fell asleep. Feeling rested, I sat quietly and watched them sleep, especially Hector. That was the first time I realized that he loved me. I've never spoken to him about that day. Perhaps one day the timing will be right and I'll remind him of his heroic act. As for me, I've long since decided there is no need to physically hear the words. Actions truly speak louder than words, and that's good enough for me.

Leticia Gómez

Love at First Sight

On a typical Saturday afternoon in 1966, I was doing the typical eleven-year-old thing—watching television—when the atypical happened. The front doorbell rang. That aroused my curiosity. No one ever came to our front door. Friends and neighbors always came around to the back.

"I'll get it," I called as I ran to see who it was. To my surprise, a young man in a blue sailor uniform stood on the porch. He cleared his throat and asked, "Is your mother home?"

I looked past him at a car parked on the street and saw three women watching through the car windows and dabbing their eyes. Turning my attention back to him, I said, "Yes, I'll get her."

Mom was in the kitchen when I told her there was a sailor asking for her. She looked up from her ironing. "A sailor?" I shrugged my shoulders.

She walked into the living room and saw him through the screen. Crying out, she threw up her arms. He rushed in and they fell into each other's embrace. The hugs and tears lasted an eternity to my young mind. I'd seen movies about sailors, and I wasn't too sure about this. Besides, Dad was in the backyard. What would he think?

Finally, Mom turned to me, her eyes red and swollen.

"Linda, this is your brother Claude."

I knew I had a brother, somewhere. Mom had told me about her marrying at a very young age to a navy man eight years her senior. She said they divorced when Claude was five years old. The divorce judge considered Mom's youth and lack of work experience and decided to award custody to Claude's father because he could better support a family. Since the divorce was a bitter one, her ex-husband moved to another state and Mom lost all contact with them. She didn't talk about it much because the memories were too painful, so I rarely thought about that part of my family history.

And now, here stood a young man of about seventeen in the living room. My brother. For me, it was love at first sight, and I ran to join the embrace.

Later that day I found out that Claude looked just like his father, and that's how Mom recognized him. He had just finished boot camp and volunteered to go to Vietnam. The navy assigned him to swift-boat training, and because he volunteered to go to war, he was awarded extra leave time.

"Momma," he said, "I made a promise to myself as a child that one day I'd find you. I knew that I might not make it back alive, and I wanted to see you before I died."

Tears fill Mom's eyes and spilled down her cheeks.

He told about the many nights he'd cried himself to sleep missing her. His father never talked about her. Claude instinctively knew it wouldn't be a good thing to mention her, either. And he vowed to find her as soon as he was old enough and on his own.

When he was told about the leave time, he asked a member of the family to help him and together they found her address. On the day of his departure, he put on his dress blues, walked to the highway, and began thumbing for a ride. The fifth car to come by pulled over. A group of women were traveling to Tennessee for a family reunion. Claude told them he was going to find his momma and they invited him to ride with them. They bought him lunch and only asked one thing of him, to let them watch his reunion from their car.

Way into the night Mom and Claude reminisced and cried. I listened, my eyes round and my mouth dry. I learned that my mom's divorce had been about her trying to escape an abusive situation with Claude's father, and that she had cried herself to sleep missing her boy. I pictured in my mind both of them in different states, crying at the same time for each other.

How I enjoyed having a brother and showing him off in his white bell-bottomed pants, but he stayed for only a few days before shipping out overseas.

While Claude served in Vietnam, we wrote back and forth. He pinned the pictures I sent to his wall and growled at any sailor who wanted my address, just like any annoying big brother should. However, I wouldn't have minded one bit showing off to my girlfriends any letters that sailors had written to me.

That was forty-one years ago. Today, no one can tell that we weren't raised together. We tease each other and talk for hours. Our lives have meshed, with nieces and nephews, grandkids, laughter, memories, and, of course, love.

When I saw that sailor in my living room, was it love at first sight? You bet. But that was only the beginning.

Linda Apple

Because of Tammi

Solitary trees, if they grow at all, grow strong.

Winston Churchill

Growing up on the Red Lake Indian Reservation in Minnesota, I didn't have much to do as a child. Luckily for me, I had a best friend to make the time better—my older sister, Tammi. We are only a year apart, and she has been there for me every step of my life. Actually, when I took my first steps, it was because of Tammi.

"Walka me baby, walka me!" That's what everyone tells me Tammi was saying as I took my first steps, walking toward her.

I never needed a friend because my best friend lived with me. I don't remember ever being bored when I was younger, and it seemed like every momentous event in my life involved Tammi. When I was three years old, for example, my mom tried to put me into Head Start. I say "tried," because I didn't stay in the program. The first day there, I cried and cried for my sister because she was in a different classroom than me.

Eight years later it was time for me to enter middle

school. Both Tammi and I had gone to Red Lake Elementary School, and she had already made the transition to middle school in a neighboring town that was forty-five minutes away. Now it was my turn to start middle school. I was so scared on my first day of sixth grade, but I was also excited because Tammi made middle school sound so cool. She was my hero during that time, because I used to think she was so cool and popular. I remember students asking, "Are you Tammi's brother?" Proudly, I'd reply, "Yes."

Middle school was also a time when we developed some differences. We were both in different "scenes." I was involved in the rock music scene and she was in the popular scene. Now, if you know anything about cliques, you know that the popular kids don't usually like to mix with the losers, so I'm sure most of Tammi's friends didn't really like me. But Tammi was one of the greatest sisters ever because she always chose me over her friends, and she stuck up for me whenever they talked about me.

I went to high school with Tammi for a year until I switched schools. At my new school, I found it so weird that I never saw her in the hallways. At my old school, I always got so excited when I saw her and I'd yell, "Hi, sister!"

Ninth grade was one of the hardest times of my life. There were the shootings at the Red Lake High School, a childhood friend committed suicide, and our grandma died. Tammi was always there to talk with me, however, and she made everything easier for me to handle.

I remember a time when I went along with my friend to pick up her brother, and for the entire ride back to her house, they didn't say a word to each other. I found this so weird, and I asked her why she didn't bother to talk with her brother. She simply told me that they just didn't talk. That was the first time I realized that not all siblings were as close as my sister and me.

Today I am sixteen and a junior in high school. Tammi is seventeen and a senior. Tammi brings me to school and picks me up every day. Every morning we eat breakfast together, which we've been doing for as long as I can remember. Next year is going to be extremely strange for me, however, because Tammi will be in college. I will be driving to school alone every day and eating breakfast alone most days. In two years, I will be going away to college, too, and I want to go to a far-away college. I have never been away from my sister for more than a week, though, and it's going to be tough. In fact, whenever I go somewhere without Tammi, people ask me where my other half is. But I know that no matter where we end up in our lives, we will always remain close.

Joe Beaulieu, age 16

My Joe

When you think of a brother/sister relationship, you probably picture a young boy and a young girl growing up together in the same home. My brother Joe and I didn't grow up in the same home at the same time.

Although we're both children of the same parents, we grew up a generation apart due to a large gap between pregnancies. My mother and father had what I call their "first family"—two boys and a girl—before I came along. The baby of the family was seventeen years old when I was born. Mom referred to me as her "surprise package," and Dad introduced me to others as his "fall crop."

Joe and I are twenty years apart. He was already grown and in the army when I entered this world. Even with the large age discrepancy, we are still siblings. I cannot say there was ever any sibling rivalry, and we never fought over toys, but he has, nevertheless, been a very important influence in my life.

My first memories of my brother were of him coming home on leave from the army. I was happy and excited when "My Joe" came home after long absences. I was only three, but my vocabulary included the names

Mama, Daddy, my puppy, and my Joe.

He would always bring me a package of Juicy Fruit gum. It may seem like nothing to others, but to me it was a very special present. That little package of Juicy Fruit made me feel special. I would chew one piece at a time, being sure not to swallow it. Mom had warned me many times about "getting stopped up" with swallowed gum. She always had a horror story about some poor little girl who swallowed too much gum. So I would chew that piece of gum for a while, then take it out of my mouth and carefully put it on the bedpost to save for the next day. That way one package of gum lasted for weeks.

While he was home, Joe also let me "drive" with him. These were the days before kids had to be strapped into a car seat and life was fun—dangerous, maybe, but fun. I "drove" Dad's Ford tractor and Joe's car. I was only three or four years old, sitting on Joe's leg and holding on tight to the steering wheel, but he had me convinced that I was the one doing the driving. "Don't go too fast. Slow down now. Okay, we are getting to the railroad track, be sure to look both ways for the train."

Joe wasn't always all fun, however, and he had a stern "fatherly" side to him. Once, when I expressed my artistic talent by using two crayons on the dining room wall, he did not appreciate my artwork at all. Although Mom, who was already a grandmother and thought it was just kid stuff, wasn't upset, Joe insisted I scrub my artistic work off the wall all by myself—art that he referred to so insensitively as "scribbling." I tried my hand at drama, too, and although I gave it my best effort, tears did not work on Joe. He was definitely hard-core.

When I was five, Joe got married. I was a flower girl in his wedding. Adorned in a pink satin dress and white patent-leather shoes, I was the picture of innocence and cuteness. I can remember all too well feeling jealous and disliking, maybe even hating, my future sister-in-law. When Joe wasn't looking, I made sure she could see me sticking my tongue out at her. I wanted her to know I did not appreciate her taking "My Joe" away from me.

As a teenager, I was a good girl. Of course, I did not have much opportunity to get into trouble. Both my parents and my grown siblings kept their eyes on me. When it came to dating, especially, all eyes were on me and it seemed like they never slept. Of course, everyone weighed in with their opinion on my first love. My sister and other brother had their doubts about this young man being a suitable partner, but Joe liked him. After I graduated from college, that first love, also known as Ben, became my husband. Ben and I are still best friends and have been happily married for thirty-three years. My brother may not have been good at recognizing artistic talent, but he was, and still is, a good judge of character.

Joe is now a father and grandfather, and although he is very busy with his immediate family, he never forgets his sis. When I turned the Big Five-O, Ben and I took a train ride to Dallas. While we were gone, I called in daily to check with my secretary, Ruby. During one call, Ruby told me that a bouquet of flowers had been delivered and asked if she should read me the card to see who sent them. I was about to tell her to go ahead—I was very curious— when she added, "And Jane, attached to the bouquet is a package of Juicy Fruit gum."

At this revelation I said, "Ruby, you don't need to open the card. I know who sent the flowers. Thanks."

I hung up the phone and began to cry. After all these years, my brother had remembered that simple little package of Juicy Fruit and, once again, it made me feel special. That's why he is "My Joe."

Jane Wiatrek

Puppy Love

Two years ago, our family went on a real long, summer car trip in our Chevy Avalanche truck. I was eight years old. It was my mom, my dad, my big sister Lahre, and me. We made a big loop through five states. From our home in California, we drove to Las Vegas and the Hoover Dam in Nevada, then to the Grand Canyon in Arizona. From there, we drove through New Mexico to Telluride, Colorado, then Salt Lake City in Utah to visit our great-grandmother. Then we headed back home through Nevada. We were gone for over two weeks.

When we were driving through the New Mexico desert on the way to Colorado, Lahre and I were getting tired of riding in the back seat. We had been arguing all day; we wanted to get out of the hot desert and into the cool Rocky Mountains of Telluride. We were going there in time for their annual Fourth of July parade and celebration, which is lots and lots of fun (this was our second time going to Telluride).

Lahre and I kept arguing about all sorts of dumb things, and then she got real mad and accidentally spilled her bottle of Gatorade all over the back seat of the truck. Dad pulled over to the side of the small highway and we got out to clean up the spill. Everyone was mad because it was so hot in the desert sun. The highway was busy, even out in the middle of nowhere.

Mom started pulling out our travel things—stuffed animals, pillows, Game Boys, snack food, books, stuff like that—from the back seat to clean up the spill. She told us to crawl up on the back of the Avalanche (the truck has a platform on the back) and wait until she finished. We were going to stand away from the truck on the side of the road, but we were afraid of any snakes or scorpions that might be out there.

Still mad at each other, we crawled up on top and waited, not talking to each other. Then Lahre saw something running down the road toward the truck. She pointed it out to me. It looked like some type of animal, but it was all blurry because of the heat waves on the road. It looked like a mirage. It came closer and closer, and we got a little scared. *Could it be a coyote?* I thought.

When it got close enough, we realized our desert animal was a little, blond puppy! It came right up to the truck and looked at us. Dad walked around the truck just in time to see the puppy. He picked it up, said it was a boy, and that it was only about seven weeks old. He put the puppy up on the truck with us and it licked us all over. Dad got a bottle of water and poured some into an upside-down Pringles chip lid. The puppy drank it up. We pleaded and begged our parents to take the puppy with us. We couldn't leave him in the desert. After we promised to behave and not argue anymore, they finally agreed.

When we started to get in the truck, the puppy went crazy and didn't want to go. Dad set him on the ground, and the puppy took off running back across the road to a bush. Dad told us to stay where we were, and he ran across the highway to the bush. When he stood up, he had two puppies in his arms! The little boy puppy had taken us to his sister. Dad brought both puppies back to the truck and said the second dog was a girl who wasn't doing very well. He handed the boy dog to Lahre and the girl dog to me. The girl dog had some water, then we all got into the truck and Dad turned on the air conditioner.

The puppies were so cute and lovable to each other. They loved each other, and it was clear that the boy dog looked after and took care of his sister. We gave them some string cheese and more water, then they both fell asleep on our laps. Lahre and I were so happy as we talked about how the puppies loved each other and took care of each other. I apologized to my big sister for getting her mad earlier, and she apologized, too. We agreed to not argue any more on the trip and that we needed to treat each other better.

When we got to the next big town on the New Mexico/ Colorado border we found a man who was sitting in a parked government truck. He turned out to be the mayor of the town! After we said a long goodbye, the mayor took the puppies, and accepted twenty dollars from Dad to help pay for some Puppy Chow. He promised to find the puppies a home together, so that they'd never be apart.

Once we got back on the road, we all laughed about our hitchhiking puppy dogs. Then we laughed more, because if Lahre and I hadn't gotten in a fight and she hadn't spilled her Gatorade, the puppies wouldn't have found us. The lesson I learned is this: It's okay to sometimes argue with your sister because something good may happen.

Shawn Shiflet, age 10

"When we were kids, you were my brother I could
tell on. Now you're my brother I can count on."

4

STORIES SHARED BY OLDER SIBLINGS

It requires wisdom to understand wisdom:
the music is nothing if the audience is deaf.

Walter Lippmann

I'll Take the Low Road

*I may not have gone where I intended to go, but
I think I have ended up where I intended to be.*

Douglas Adams

Last year, my family spent Christmas at my parents'
house. When our relatives get together, it's a madhouse.
Mom and Dad are foster parents, and there are always
kids everywhere, playing videos, running in and out of
the house, watching television, or right underfoot in the
kitchen where people are trying to cook.

My dad and brother Brad sat at the kitchen table so
they could visit with the cooks. We ladies (the cooks)
wanted them to help corral the children. Occasionally,
they would catch one before they actually made it into the
kitchen-cooking chaos.

Brian, my four-year-old magician, snatched food then
magically disappeared before anyone could reprimand
him. My seventeen-year-old daughter, Amanda, was
doing the same. Frustrated, I asked her to take her
brother out into the beautiful December day and play
catch with him.

Suddenly, my brother Brad jumped up from his seat. "That's not such a good idea," he said. "I'll keep Brian out of the kitchen." Lifting Brian onto his shoulders, he shouted, "Everyone outside to play ball!"

Mom and I looked at each other, bewildered. *Wasn't that what I had just suggested?* I thought.

Later, as we all sat around the table for dessert, I asked Brad, "Why did you jump up and take the kids outside after disagreeing with my idea about playing catch?"

"Let me tell you a story about a little boy and his big sister," he said.

"There once was a little boy who looked up to his sister. She was six years older than him. He'd watch her playing outside with all her friends, wishing she'd play with him, too.

"He'd sit on the curb and watch as she played catch with a neighborhood friend, or ride her bike and do jumps. He'd watch as she did cartwheels in the yard and then tell him he couldn't do cartwheels because he was a boy. She would play tag with her friends and tell him he was too little and too slow to play with them. 'Just leave me and my friends alone,' she'd say. So, the little boy would hang his head, go into the house, and pout.

"But his mom, being a smart mom, would always know. His mom would say, 'Play with your brother!' Rolling her eyes, the sister would grab her ball and glove and stomp out the door. The little boy would be elated, even knowing what was coming next.

"His sister would claim the upper part of the street and he would take the lower, which ran downhill. The boy was always so excited. It was hard for him to throw the ball the way he knew he should. All he knew was that *finally* his big sister was playing with him. One minute he was grinning and bursting with pride because his sister was playing ball with him, and the next he was chasing the ball all the way down the hill. He knew he had to hurry or she might get mad that he was being slow. He'd chase the ball and finally catch up with it. Triumphantly, he'd turn with it in his upraised hand, the grin still on his face, only to see that no one was there. His sister had deserted him!"

As my brother's story unfolded, I wondered why it was beginning to sound a little too familiar.

"No matter how many times this story was replayed," my brother continued, "each time the same thing happened, and it broke the little boy's heart. Still, he always looked forward to playing ball with his sister, even if it meant only five minutes of fun. It was worth it to him because he adored her so much."

"What an awful little girl," I said. "I'm beginning to get the picture and understand why you didn't want Amanda to play catch with her brother."

My sister looked at me with a knowing grin, and my brother had a twinkle in his eye. Visions of my little brother sitting on the curb watching me play catch with my friends came rushing into my memory. I remembered how he would watch me play tag. I felt sad, and tears filled my eyes. Overwhelmed with remorse, I regretted the kind of sister I had been. How I wished I could go back and do things differently.

I've given it a lot of thought, and I've decided that perhaps there were times I could have been kinder to my brother and sister. Most people could say the same. I remember our parents telling us: "Friends will come and go throughout your life. But your brother and sister will always be there for you. So, be nice to them, and look out for each other."

On that Christmas day, surrounded by all our children, we retold childhood experiences. Some brought tears, others laughter. After clearing away the dessert dishes, I grabbed three baseball gloves. Keeping one, I tossed one to my brother and the other to my sister.

"Let's go play some ball," I offered. "And I'll take the bottom of the hill this time."

Vivian M. Johnson

The height of sibling rivalry.

Chuckie

It was Saturday morning. Driving down the street as usual, a little faster than I should, I glanced at my "To Do" list. For the last three years, I've always started the day with my "To Do" list. It helps me get organized and stay focused, and I get a feeling of power and accomplishment when each completed chore is crossed off the list.

But today I was running behind and I still had to stop at the grocery store and dry cleaners. I pulled into the grocery store lot and lucked out, easily finding a parking space. *Shouldn't take too long . . . I only have to buy a few things,* I thought. I shopped quickly and went to the express checkout counter. To my dismay, the person in front of me had more than ten items. *I guess the person can't read! This is an express aisle!*

It was already 1:00 PM, but I assured myself that I would not miss my Saturday afternoon date. *I won't have time to pick up the dry cleaning,* I sighed to myself. That would have to be the first thing on Monday's "To Do" list. Finally, I was able to get out of the store with my grocery bag and headed home, thinking about my list.

When I got home, I put the groceries away. Life was just as hectic in the house with my busy family buzzing around.

Busy as things were, however, it was time to go on my date with Chuckie. I said good-bye to my husband and kids. I shut my cell phone off, and said, "I'll be back in two or three hours."

Chuckie is my forty-five-year-old brother. He was born with Down syndrome that caused severe retardation and has been living in a nearby group home for over ten years. I began these weekly dates because our mother, may she rest in peace, always expressed concern for Chuckie. I assured her I would look after him.

When I arrived at the home that day, Chuckie was sitting in the living room waiting for me. As usual, he was happy to see me. "My sister is here," he announced, with unconditional love on his face. I didn't have to worry about what I looked like or if I was late; the joy on Chuckie's face was worth it.

"Okay Chuckie, are you ready to go for a ride?"

"Ready," he said.

Chuckie loves cars, long rides, and listening to the radio. We share a favorite oldie's station, and we always sing along. I am not blessed with a good voice, so the only time I sing my heart out, loud and clear, is when I drive around with Chuckie. He is the only one who enjoys my singing.

"Would you like to stop for an ice cream, Chuck?"

"Yeah, chocolate!"

My heart warmed again, thinking that it is so easy to please him. We got our ice cream then headed to the park to walk around and enjoy nature. After a bit, we saw a bench and decided to rest for a while. While relaxing, I took out photos from my handbag and together we looked at pictures of our family. Chuck identified each person with joy. There were photos of Mom and Dad when they were young, and of Chuckie and me when we were kids. He even enjoyed photos of our grandmother. I was surprised that he remembered Grandmom since she had been dead for over thirty years; however, she was a big part of our lives as children.

Sitting in the park with my brother, a peace and tranquility came over me. My "ToDo" list seemed so unimportant, and my stressful week and hustle-bustle morning are forgotten. I like to think that Chuckie's purpose on this Earth is to be a force of beauty and innocence in a fast-moving, complicated world. In some small way, bits of those traits, like rays of sunshine, touch the people he encounters.

The afternoon passed too quickly, and it was time to take Chuckie back to the group home. In the car, we both sang "Let It Be" by the Beatles. When I dropped him off, we went through our usual ritual. I hugged him tightly.

"Love you, Chuckie."

"Love you, too," he said. Then he asked, "See ya next Saturday?"

"Wouldn't miss it for the world, Chuckie." He smiled as he watched me leave, and I looked in the rear-view mirror and noticed he was still smiling as I drove away.

The afternoon with my brother was a nice respite, but I knew my euphoric feeling wouldn't last too long. By tomorrow, I'd probably be feeling somewhat stressed, but I would look forward to my next date with Chuckie, when I would be reminded to slow down and enjoy the beauty in the world.

Lucille Engro DiPaolo

Frosty the Snowman

Nobody ever died of laughter.

Max Beerbohm

My family and I live about two hours from several Sierra Nevada ski resorts, and we love to ski. The snow was perfect the day we chose to take the short drive "up the hill" from Sacramento, and with no storms blowing in, it turned out to be a sunny and warm day with almost no wind.

My father is an excellent skier, and so he went on some very hard runs by himself, while my stepmother, Michelle, my little brother, Shawn, and I headed for some easier runs. We took one of the chairlifts up the hill and got off at the top, turning to the right, which was a "beginner's" run. For my little brother Shawn, it was a big hill; for Michelle and me, it was a piece of cake. All three of us started skiing down the mountain, but suddenly Shawn somehow got turned around and was skiing down backward! He was screaming, "Mommy! Lahre! Help!"

I was below him, so I stopped, took off my skis, and ran up the mountain. He grabbed me and held on for dear life.

"Shawn, it's okay, bud, I got you," I tried to assure him. I turned him around so he was facing forward, but he was still so scared and crying a little. I really wanted to find a way to make my little brother smile and laugh. I wanted him to know how much fun skiing could be, and I wanted him to have fun skiing the rest of the day. I ran back down to my skis and put them on. Shawn was still upset and scared as the three of us continued down the hill.

Then I saw it, my opportunity to make my brother laugh. Sitting there, right in the middle of the run, was a snowman! I was so excited because I pictured myself skiing through the snowman and its fluffy snow flying all over me. It would just be so cool! As I picked up speed, heading downhill directly at the snowman, I screamed to my little brother, "Shawn, watch this!"

Just as I was expecting to hit the snowman and send it flying into a billion snowy pieces, my skis hit what had turned into a snowman-shaped solid block of ice. Instead of the snowman flying everywhere, my right ski popped off and went flying in one direction while I flew over the snowman and continued tumbling and sliding down the hill in the other direction.

When I finally opened my eyes, I was lying on my back and everything was quiet. Then I heard them—Shawn and Michelle—laughing so hard! I had gotten my wish: Shawn was happy and laughing. Skiing was once again fun for my little brother.

Lahre Shiflet, age 15

Hung Up

What lies behind us and what lies before us are tiny matters compared to what lies within us.

Ralph Waldo Emerson

If I had known what would happen to my brother, I never would have left the house. But I had finished practicing my piano, and the Oklahoma sunshine called me outside. I slipped out the back door and hurried toward the pasture—my place of refuge.

As a teenager, I needed my time alone to think about boys or my life's purpose or how to get into the right college. I cherished my alone time, and I knew I needed to hurry or my brother would follow me. As I ran toward my favorite retreat, a shadow moved into my peripheral vision.

Phil, my brother, was climbing over the barbed wire fence, intent on following me. At ten, he was deep into the larva stage of manhood and delighted in sneaking up on his sister. A goofy grin now spread across his face as he swung one leg over the top wire.

"Go away," I yelled. "I want to be alone."

He didn't answer, but kept climbing. I started to run into another part of the pasture when I heard him yelp, accompanied by the sound of ripping cloth.

Looking back, I saw Phil on the ground, clutching his leg. All thoughts of being alone disappeared as I ran toward him. A two-foot gash ran down the length of his leg where the barbed wire had separated blue jeans from flesh. Blood was already dripping onto the ground beneath him.

"Okay, give me your hand," I said. After hoisting him to his feet, I wrapped his arm around my neck and grabbed his belt with my other hand. We hopped and slid back to the house.

Mom came quickly when I yelled for her. After one look at the wound, our nurse mother pushed us into the car for a quick trip to the emergency room. "Just once," she said to Phil, "I'd like you to get a tetanus shot at the doctor's office rather than the ER."

At the hospital, Mom held Phil's hand while the doctor cut off the rest of his jeans, cleansed the wound, and started suturing the flesh together. I stood in the corner, trying not to cry and wishing a thousand times that I had helped my little brother over the fence rather than trying to run away from him.

He flinched a few times, but didn't cry as the doctor injected painkillers and ended the ordeal with a new tetanus shot. My stomach roiled at the sights and smells, and I decided on the spot to never pursue a medical degree. I felt proud of my brave little brother and promised myself I would be kinder to him.

Afterward, Mom treated us to ice cream then drove us home. Once again, Phil wore that goofy grin as I patted his good leg. He got what he wanted most, to be with his big sister.

R. J. Thesman

Deserving of a Name

When I was only eight years old, my mom gave birth to my new baby brother: Britt Ashford Reice Wilson. I have always been jealous of him and his extra name; after all, I only have three names!

Britt was the youngest of six children and was born with some special medical needs, just like my little sister, Alanna. The Children's Hospital in Milwaukee was pretty much their home for months following their births.

Later on, Britt became very sick and had been in the hospital for about four months. When the doctors realized the hospital wasn't helping much, they let him come home for a little while. During the end of his home visit, I was invited to go stay with my friend a few hours north of us. I accepted quite eagerly. The plan was for me to stay for about two weeks. I was so excited. All I ever talked about was her house and how much fun we always had.

The night before I left, we kids had a camp-out in the living room. We had a television and everything. We always let Britt choose the movies that we watched. That night, he just happened to choose *What a Girl Wants*. Sitting side by side— Britt, Alanna, Quinton, and me—we laughed throughout the movie. Eventually, we all fell asleep with it still on.

The next morning, I was in a hurry to get ready: pack my toothbrush, eat breakfast—it was all such a bother! When my friend arrived to pick me up, I ran outside and hopped in the car without saying good-bye to anyone. For some odd reason, my mom came running out, calling my name, and telling me to say good-bye to Britt. I ran back inside, hugged him, kissed him, and told him that I loved him. He replied, "I love you, Noly. Bye!"

I had been at my friend's house for only three days when my dad called. It was a beautiful summer day, and I had just gotten out of the pool. Dad told me something was wrong: Britt had died that morning. He choked on his vomit because he didn't have the strength to push it out of his mouth. Tears welled up in my eyes, and I pretended that I had no clue what he had just said, even though I did. I just thought maybe if I didn't accept it right away, the words would change. They didn't. I cried for the next two hours, and I cried myself to sleep that night.

When I got home, I found that everyone was a mess. *If everyone is crying, who will manage the house?* I thought. I felt I had to be strong for the family, so I cried once, for maybe five minutes, at the funeral. Otherwise, not once did a tear fall from my cheek. My mom thought that I didn't care, but what she didn't know was that I cared very much. I felt like I wasn't part of the family much anymore because I hadn't been there when Britt died.

Now, each year becomes a little easier to handle, but I love him just as much. Britt was only three and a half when he died, and it's been two years. Every now and then, I feel a tap on my shoulder or someone brush up against me, but when I turn around, there's not a soul there. That's when I realize that it's Britt. He visits to say, "Noly, even though I'm in heaven, it doesn't mean that I'm not with you. I love you and can't wait to see you on the other side."

I now realize why Britt received his extra name. It wasn't because my parents loved him more, but because he had been made a little more special and with a little more love, since he wouldn't be around as long. If it had been up to me, I would've given him ten names. He deserved them.

Nolyn Wilson, age 13

Never Say Never

It is better to know some of the questions than all of the answers.

James Thurber

"The doctor says I could die if I have another child."

My mother told me this when I was twelve. So during her pregnancy, when she swelled up and turned yellow, I panicked. I thought she was a goner, and that the baby was to blame.

On June 4, 1970, my brother was born prematurely. It would be weeks before he could come home, and I waited nervously to see the thing that had caused so much trouble. But when he arrived and they unraveled his blankets, exposing his little, naked body, I laughed. With his bloated belly, skinny limbs, and rashy skin, he resembled a wrinkled, red frog. I realized as he lay there—small, frail, and crying—that he was no longer a threat, so I devoted myself to his constant care. I fed him, changed him, rubbed him with baby oil, and doused him with talcum powder. I nurtured and protected him. And with great defiance, I never let anyone cut his hair.

Over time, he blossomed into a bubbly little boy with soft, blond curls and big, blue eyes—one of which got covered with a black pirate's patch to strengthen the *other* eye, which a doctor had deemed lazy because it always turned inward, looking at his nose.

By the summer of 1975, we had become quite the sibling duo. He was five, I was eighteen. He was short, I was tall. He wore a pirate's patch and had a lazy eye, and I wore bellbottoms with bare feet. And we both had long hair. Then, because we were two restless rebels in pursuit of a pastime, I bought a clunker of a car and named it Daisy.

She was a faded blue, 1964 Chevy Malibu with bench seats, bald tires, and a scab of rust on her hood. To boot, she had an eight-track player connected to a pair of blown-out speakers. And though she guzzled as much oil as gas, she gave my brother and me the freedom to explore the world—within a certain radius of our house.

My brother, old Daisy, and I spent many carefree days cruising suburbia to the crackling sounds of Pink Floyd and enjoying curb service at the local Steak-n-Shake, sipping orange freezes and splitting grilled cheese sandwiches.

Months later on a cold night in December, my mother and I got into a screaming match that ended with her telling me to get out and never come back. I, in turn, informed her that I had already planned to leave (a lie) and had a place to go (a bigger lie), and I would never come back! I packed Daisy with a basket of clothes and left.

About two weeks later, I got a call at work. It was my brother and it was his first time using a phone. Someone must have helped him dial the number.

In his little boy voice he inquired about my new living arrangements.

"You got food?"

"Yes."

"You got a house?

"No."

"You got a bed?

I started to cry. "Daisy is my bed."

Shocked, he asked, "You sleep on Daisy?"

"No, silly," I said, laughing through my tears. "I sleep inside, on the seat."

"Oh," he giggled, and then reported to someone on his end, "She sleeps in Daisy."

All along, I had been sleeping in my car on the next street over, where I could still see our house. But in below-freezing temperatures, without covers or a coat, I practically froze to death.

After more muffled conversation between my brother and one of my parents, he scolded me. "You need to come home and sleep in your real bed, the one in your room."

On Christmas morning I came home. My family was in the living room unwrapping presents. There were none under the tree for me. My brother, sitting on his new Big Wheel in the middle of torn wrapping paper and battered boxes, noticed the oversight.

"Guess Santa couldn't find you," he offered.

I felt awkward, as did my parents. Not only had we not yet spoken to one another, we hadn't even made eye contact. Instead, we watched my brother. He climbed into my lap and cupped my face with his tiny hands. "Are you going to sleep in your real bed tonight?" he asked.

"I think so," I said, unsure if my parents wanted me to stay.

Still cupping my face, he became very serious. "Then can I . . . ," he moved in closer, his little, lazy eye trying to focus, until we were nearly nose to nose, " . . . then can I sleep in Daisy?"

We broke out in laughter. My parents and I joked about the need for parkas and electric blankets with long extension cords. The laughing led to hugging, then to tears, then to forgiveness and finally peace. My parents left the room and returned with a beautifully wrapped gift. My brother and I were surprised, and as I opened it, he exclaimed, "Santa knows you're home!" I lifted out a fluffy, white coat, with fake fur trim on the hood and cuffs. Although it was unlike the hippie attire I usually sported, it was perfect.

That night, while Daisy sat parked in front of our house with frost-covered windows, my little brother and I slept soundly in our toasty, warm beds . . . in the house, together.

Patsy Zettler

Snapping Turtles Beware

Donny was always the inquisitive one. And for that I think I loved him the most. At three, Donny was the second youngest in our clan of seven. I was the second oldest at eleven. I loved being with the younger children, tending to them while Momma worked hard in the house.

Everywhere I went, little brother Donny followed. He was forever looking for a new adventure. He'd have me out in the yard chasing after grasshoppers or fireflies. It didn't matter what he was doing—he loved life to the fullest. I can still picture him with his straight blond hair, big blue eyes, and a smile that would melt my heart.

"Feed ducks, Tammy!" his squeaky little voice said.

I smiled down at him and tousled his hair. "Okay, we can go feed the ducks."

I gathered little sisters Maggie and Dawn and off to the pond we went, carrying old bread that Momma had saved for us.

It was a beautiful August day, the sun shining brightly in the sky. There were no clouds, and it wasn't too hot. Maggie and Dawn took off chasing each other, while Donny hung by my side, throwing bread for the geese and ducks.

"Tickles," Donny said after the goose nipped a piece of bread from his chubby little fingers.

"Yes, it does." I gave my little brother a big hug. "Are you having fun?" I knew the answer already, but I wanted to hear his reassurance.

"Uh-huh," he said shaking his head up and down quickly. "Can I go swimming?"

"No, Donny. We're not allowed to swim in the pond."

"How come?" he asked, hands on hips.

"There are snapping turtles in the pond. You wouldn't want them to bite your toes, would you?"

Eyes wide, he replied, "No way!" I giggled, hoping that would cure his desire to swim.

"Tammy, look!" Maggie called from a few yards away. She stood pointing to the ground. I headed toward the girls, never once wondering if Donny was following because that's what he did.

When I reached the girls, I looked at what held their interest. Lying on the ground was a baby duck. It didn't look too healthy, and no mother was in sight to tend the duckling. As I bent over to examine it, the girls' mouths moving a mile a minute with questions, a little voice went off in my head. *Where's Donny?* By now he would have been bent over, too, wanting to take care of the duckling himself.

I jumped up and spun around calling for my little brother. "Donny! Where are you Donny?" Panic set in.

"Girls, did you notice Donny following me?"

"No," they said in unison.

"We need to find him *now!*"

Fear seized me as I realized what he had done. I ran straight for the pond. Without hesitation I ran into the water searching for Donny. I felt around for his body. At age three he didn't know how to swim. He only knew he wanted to go into the water.

Tears streaming down my face I dove underwater and finally found him. I pulled his lifeless body up and out of the water. He was heavy, but I clung to him for dear life. I looked for the girls on shore, but now they were gone, too. *Dear God, please tell me they aren't in the pond,* I cried inside. As I trudged through the water that felt as thick as mud, my plan was to get Donny to safety, then go back in and look for my sisters.

I spread Donny out on the hard ground and brushed my hand over his cold cheeks. "Please, dear God, don't take my brother from me yet. I love him so much."

At that instant I heard the girls yelling, "There he is. Please save him!" They had a man with them.

Relief washed over me when I realized that they had run for help and not followed me into the water. The girls were safe, and maybe even heroes for bringing someone to help their brother.

The scene felt surreal. I watched the man pushing on my brother's frail chest, pinching his nose, and breathing into his mouth. Wringing my hands, I silently prayed. The girls were clinging to me, crying for Donny to live. I couldn't console them. I could only think about Donny.

As water choked out of Donny's mouth, I fell to the ground placing kisses all over his head and face. The sound of a siren could be heard as it grew closer and closer. An ambulance arrived to take Donny to the hospital, where he made a full recovery. When I saw him in the oversized bed, tubes hooked up to him, tears formed in my eyes.

Donny smiled. "I don't like snapping turtles," he said weakly.

Tina O'Reilly

Carnival Daze

Those who bring sunshine to the lives of others cannot keep it from themselves.

James Barrie

I heard five-year-old Richard's voice as he flew through the house screaming, "The carnival is here! The carnival is here!"

Summer had finally arrived. All winter we had dreamt of summer and the carnival. Three nights of bright lights and loud noises meant summer fun had arrived and we could finally crawl out from under the blanket of our cold, snowy winters.

I grabbed my jacket and raced out the door. I had to see this with my own eyes. I loved to watch as the muscle men built the rides straight out of the huge semi-trucks they drove. Their electrical cords twisted and coiled over the ground, tripping any small feet that ventured out. Last year I tripped over one and fell flat in a mud puddle. My friends never let me forget it.

We lived three blocks away and could hear the heavy machines of the carnival rides as they heaved and tossed their riders into the air. Joyous screams filled the night air. The smell of cotton candy, caramel-covered apples, greasy hamburgers, and hot dogs pierced the evenings. What scrumptious smells!

Saturday finally arrived and so did the planned meeting with my friends after the town parade. I had forgotten that my mom wanted me to let my little brother tag along behind me.

"You big baby, why do I always have to take you around everywhere I go?" I glared at him. He looked away and got teary eyed.

"Oh, stop crying. I'll take you around so you don't miss any rides." A twinge of guilt washed over me. I was being so mean to Richard, but I wanted to be with my friends, not with him riding the baby rides.

"I want to go on that one." He was pointing to the big fire truck going around on the small track.

"Go then!" I shoved Richard toward the ride. I followed him at a distance. He got on the ride and pointed his finger back at me. *No way! I wasn't getting on a kiddy ride where everyone would see me,* I thought. Richard kept pointing his finger at me, and the ride attendant motioned me to come over. I stomped over, shaking my head.

"Just get on for your little brother. He's holding up the line," the attendant barked.

"No way!" I hollered and looked at Richard in disbelief.

"Then I'll have to take him off the ride," he said.

I couldn't believe this. He was really going to make me ride this ride. *I'm thirteen years old. I'm too old for this ride. I'm too big for this ride.* The attendant made a move to take Richard off.

"Hold on," I said as guilt overwhelmed me. I didn't want my brother to miss the ride. His eyes were pleading with me to get on. He was going to pay for this; I'd make him do all my chores for a whole month.

I climbed into the little fire truck and sat down next to Richard. He was grinning from ear to ear and patting my hand. The ride started and we began going round and round. I looked out into the crowd as it gathered for the next turn and was utterly embarrassed to see Tom Robertson standing by the fence looking at me. He was only the cutest boy in school. There he stood with his group of friends. My best friend, Amy, had said he liked me. I was mortified to have him see me riding this baby ride. *What would he think of me now?* I tried to turn my head as the fire truck approached him. I put my hand up and turned my back toward the fence, but it was too late— he'd seen me. His friends pointed at me, and I heard them laughing. Oh, how my brother was going to pay dearly for this humiliation.

"You owe me two months of chores," I said through gritted teeth.

He looked up and his smile faded. "You don't want to ride with me?"

I was stunned. He actually thought I wanted to ride this with him. I felt like a heel.

"Kids my age don't ride the kiddy-car ride. We're too big," I tried to sound convincing and grown-up.

He stared at me. "You used to ride this one with me all the time." I felt worse than ever. The ride ended and we hurried out of the fence. I wanted to get away as quickly as possible. I ran into Tom just as we rounded the corner.

"Hey, nice ride you were on," he snickered.

"Yeah it was a nice one. Have you tried it?" I said sarcastically. I was mad that he would try to make fun of me. "My brother begged me to ride it with him and I just couldn't say no."

"Yeah, me neither," said Tom. "My baby sister wants me to ride it with her. I told her I didn't want to and she cried for half an hour. Maybe it's not so bad after all."

Tom Robertson thought it was a cool idea? Wow! Maybe I could set a trend for the other big brothers and sisters in town, I thought.

"If you're around later on, do you want to go on some rides together?" Tom asked.

"Sure. I need to go ride more with my little brother. Meet you back here at five?" I smiled at him as he nodded, and as we brushed passed each other, our arms touched. I felt a tingle shoot to my head.

"Richard, want to go on some more rides together?" I asked as I grabbed my little brother's hand and began walking toward more kiddy rides.

Cindy Ovard

Brother by Choice

Other things may change us, but we start and end with the family.

Anthony Brandt

"Watch out for the shark!" my ten-year-old cousin Sean shrieked. "It's a big one!" I scanned the water, searching its murky darkness for the monster lurking beneath.

"I see it," I breathed as the great, grey shadow slid by me.

"You'll have to jump," said Sean as he paced on the safety of the boat deck. "You're sinking." He pointed to the stern of my boat, which was dangerously low in the dark seawaters.

I felt the wetness licking at my ankles and took a deep breath. Closing my eyes, I vaulted myself over the side of the boat and prayed that I would make it to safety.

I landed on the champagne-colored couch with a grunt and dissolved into gales of laughter. Undone, Sean fell too, and together we howled at the hilarity of it all.

"What's going on in there?" Grandma called from the kitchen. Smiling, she poked her head into her formal living room, where blanket forts and the cushions from her Victorian toile sofa surrounded the two of us.

My mother would have been surprised. She had often told us that as children she and her younger sister, Sally, were forbidden to play in their mother's formal living room. Apparently, Grandma had mellowed with age; she actually seemed amused by our games. It may have been Sean's presence. He was the "golden child" in the family, and the only boy among the grandchildren. For Grandma, the small, red-haired boy, who was grinning at me from his side of the pretend boat, could do no wrong.

He tossed her one of his impish smiles and she lovingly nodded at him and went back to the kitchen.

"So, what should we do next?" he asked eagerly.

Although he was clearly spoiled, I was never jealous of Sean. He was a great friend, an enthusiastic playmate, and he had no problem sharing the mountain of toys he always got at Christmas. Despite his status as the favorite, his life had not been easy. Four years earlier, his father left Sean and his mother to fend for themselves. It was difficult, because Sean's mother—my Aunt Sally—was ill. Crohn's disease had ravaged her small body, leaving her unable to work. The two of them depended largely on family to survive. They lived in a small apartment down the street from Grandma and Grandpa's house, and when his mother was ill, Sean spent a great deal of time with the rest of us.

One morning, Sean awoke and found that his mother had passed away during the night. She had been sick for years. Conceiving him had been a miracle, and carrying him had been an amazing feat. She had been broken by miscarriages many times, brought on by her illness, and when Sean was born six weeks early, he was sickly and wasn't expected to live. He was her heart, and she had been his champion. Now she was gone. Little Sean sat by her bedside, sobbing for most of the day. He didn't know what to do, and it wasn't until Grandma had dropped by later in the afternoon that any of us knew Aunt Sally had passed away.

I remember watching Sean during her funeral. His clear blue eyes had been clouded with pain and confusion. I was only three years older than him; I didn't fully understand what he was going through. His father had abandoned him, and now the person he loved most in the world had been taken from him. My heart ached to think of the pain he must have been feeling.

Sean went to live with Grandma. Grandpa had died earlier in the year, and now with the loss of her youngest daughter, she welcomed the company. We all thought that perhaps the two of them would mend their broken hearts together. Unfortunately, the loss of her loved ones proved too much, and stress-induced dementia took the Grandma we had known and loved from us as well.

That was when Sean came to live with us. He was eleven and I was fourteen. He was lost. The smiling, laughing boy I had always known was now quiet and scared. He didn't know where he belonged, and the people who had meant the most to him were gone. We were all he had left. I wondered if we would ever be enough.

It wasn't long before I considered Sean my brother. In my heart, that's who he was. I loved him fiercely. I didn't know if he felt the same—he called my mom and dad "Aunt" and "Uncle." I wondered if, in his heart, he still belonged to those who were gone. I didn't want to make him uncomfortable, but I wanted him to know how I felt.

I decided the next time I introduced him to someone, I would say, "This is my brother Sean." The opportunity came soon after, and after I said the words, I waited for his reaction.

I need not have worried. Sean heard the words and smiled, rewarding me with that grin I remembered. I smiled back and said nothing more. I had a brother and Sean had a sister, and despite all that we had lost, what we had gained was immeasurable—family.

Recently, Sean received word that his biological father had passed away. Confused and unsure how to feel about the death of a man who had been gone from his life for years, his voice cracked when he told me the news.

"I'm an orphan," he said.

I looked at him and shook my head. "No," I said quietly. "You belong to me."

He smiled then, not the boy I remembered, but the man he had become. Every tragedy that had befallen him had helped make him the person he was, a person I was proud to know. Blood may be thicker than water, but the ties that bind do not know the difference.

This is my brother—not by blood, but by choice.

Julie Henry

5

LOVING HANDS

Do all things with love.

Og Mandino

A Real-Life Prince

*It is not true that nice guys finish last. Nice guys
are winners before the game ever starts.*

Addison Walker

It was one week before my senior prom, and my universe had just imploded.

You see, as eight out of ten female high school seniors will tell you (and nine out of ten secretly believe), your final high school prom is only slightly less significant than your wedding day. It should be as romantic and dramatic as Cinderella's ball, which is only natural, since every prom-going girl expects to *be* Cinderella for a night. And of course, the magic all begins in that enchanted moment when your Prince Charming extends the invitation.

So there I was, with prom just one week away, facing the unimaginable—the guy that everybody (including me) had assumed would be my prom date had suddenly asked someone else. It wasn't a betrayal, strictly speaking. He wasn't my boyfriend, but he *was* my best buddy and besides, he should have *known*. There are certain immutable truths about senior prom that everybody should intuitively understand. All the girls certainly did. Even worse, as I mentally scanned my repertoire of potential Prince Charmings hoping to find a last-minute date, I realized that they had long since done right by their Cinderellas-to-be. I was without a date, without even a prospective date, and the future looked bleak indeed.

My older brother, Darren, had just returned from college, but even in my desperation, going to the prom with my brother never crossed my mind. There are certain standards that you just don't violate. And since he had graduated three years earlier, and all of his friends were spread across the country, he wasn't a likely resource to help solve my problem. But in my self-absorbed teenage angst, I had temporarily forgotten a fundamental truth that had always lent structure to my life: my family was my one reliable safety net in times of crisis. So it came as a genuine surprise when I returned from school one day to find Darren anxious to share the good news: he had arranged for one of his longtime friends to drive up for the weekend and take me to the prom.

Although my initial reaction was still pretty self-centered—relief at being spared this fate worse than death, and trying to remember if Darren's friend was taller than me—it didn't take long for me to snap out of Cinderella mode and realize that I was actually experiencing something *more* significant (gasp!) than my prom. Even more than by the remarkable unselfishness of Darren's friend, who only remembered me as a kid sister, I was sincerely touched by my brother's concern over my unhappiness. Somewhat ashamed at my previous ego-centricity, I tried to make it right. I called one of my girlfriends and asked if she would like to accompany my brother, hoping that a double date would make the situation more comfortable for my borrowed Prince Charming, and hoping that Darren would have a fun evening, too.

Darren did have a fun evening—all four of us did. And as eight out of ten thirty-something women will tell you (except those who have high-school daughters of their own, because they know they would never be believed), it's now hard to imagine how my prom could have had even the tiniest impact on my current life. However, it did turn out to be a night my brother would never forget. By proving himself a real-life Prince Charming to me, he made a karmic investment that paid off in a big way. Exactly one year later, his blind date to his little sister's prom became his fiancée, then his wife. Now that she's been my sister-in-law for eighteen years, we often reflect on how glad we are that my original high school Cinderella fantasy *didn't* come true!

Lisa Davenport Freeman

"As first born, you must take on the responsibility
of leading your younger brothers and sisters."

Love in the Air

   As children, my three older brothers and I squabbled as often as any kids do. I suffered from their disdain. I cried when they teased me. I threatened to tell Mom.

   I remember a particularly frustrating time when I was twelve. Mom was away for a month caring for her aging mother. She left me in charge of preparing all meals, washing the clothes, and cleaning the house. One Saturday morning, I added a double portion of soap powder to the load of laundry by mistake. Soon bubbles were frothing higher and higher. I closed the washer lid but the bubbles squeezed out the edges and slid down the sides of the machine onto the floor. In a panic, I called to my oldest brother, Richard, for help.

   Richard entered the laundry room, surveyed the situation, and then offered his sage advice: "If I were you, I wouldn't put in so much soap." No offer to assist me in cleaning up the mess. No sympathy for my plight. Just this wisdom: "Don't put in as much soap next time."

   Still, despite all the frustrations, as Richard and I grew older, we also grew closer. I missed him when he left home for college in California. Four years later, I left for a campus on the opposite side of the country. At college, I faced big decisions. I was majoring in anthropology, but was it the right major? I was dating a young man steadily, and we were talking about marriage, but was he really the person I wanted to be with for the rest of my life?

Richard became aware of my confusion. This time, instead of sage advice, he offered to pay for my airplane flight from New York to Los Angeles so I could attend a special conference. This wasn't an easy choice for him. He had just graduated from college and had no extra money in the bank. But by giving me that trip to California, away from all the pressures of school, I was able to view my life more clearly. I decided to keep my college major, but break off the relationship with my boyfriend. Those two decisions had an enormous impact on my life. And a year later, I met the man to whom I am now married.

The years sped by. Richard left to work in Greece, and I worked for several years in Mexico before returning to the States to marry my husband. Because of geography, I didn't get to see Richard very often.

In 1979, my second brother planned to fly from California to the East Coast with his wife and children for the Christmas holiday. We looked forward to meeting his newest child, Heather, the first female grandchild in the family. Because this was a difficult trip for his family, we realized such an opportunity for a family reunion might not come up again for several years. My parents and my youngest brother arranged to rendezvous with my husband and myself at our home in Pennsylvania.

But what about Richard? My oldest brother was still in Greece. He had no funds to pay for an extra holiday visit to the States. Then my husband, Gene, suggested that we buy Richard's airline ticket home and make it our surprise gift to the whole family.

I exclaimed, "A ticket would cost hundreds of dollars!"

We were not rich. As newlyweds, Gene and I spent

money very carefully. Christmas was such a short holiday, and Richard was already planning to return to the States the following summer. I could think of many reasons why buying a plane ticket was impractical, but because we really wanted Richard to be with us, my husband went ahead and purchased the ticket.

Richard arrived at the airport late one wintry night in December before the rest of the family arrived. The next day, still overcoming jet lag, he greeted Mom and Dad at the door when they drove in from Virginia. Their smiles of surprise were brighter than any tinsel on the tree. What a joy to have all their children together for the first time in many years! We asked a photographer to take a family portrait to document the occasion. Little Heather slept on her mother's lap—front and center.

The days sped by and soon everyone was bundling into coats, saying good-byes, and climbing into cars. We drove Richard to the airport.

Later that day, as I piled sheets and towels into the washer (with the right amount of detergent) and folded the last bits of holiday wrapping paper, I wondered once again if we had spent our money wisely. Little did I know that Christmas 1979 was the last time our entire family would ever be together. Shortly after the New Year, my second brother entered a hospital where he remained for several years. During that period our mother died. We never again had the opportunity to come together as a complete family, not even at her funeral.

When I was in college, Richard had invested in a plane ticket that affected my life in ways he couldn't have imagined. In 1979, my husband and I bought a plane ticket for Richard, which gave our family a memory that we could never purchase again. Each expression of love involved a large investment, but both netted long-term rewards.

Emily Parke Chase

Always the Protector

I was eight years old when I experienced my first bicycle accident: my knee versus the gravel road. The doctor sutured my bleeding knee as my brother K.W. stood close by, carefully watching. I'd like to think it was an act of genuine brotherly concern, but I suspect it may have just been that medicine fascinated him. Still, at the time, I viewed it as the valiant deed of an older brother looking out for his younger sister.

Three years later, our mother died. I was eleven and K.W. was twelve. Our father had died six years earlier, and with the passing of our mother, we became orphans and were sent to live with relatives in different states.

Despite the fact that we missed some of the most important years of sibling bonding, we did keep in touch and shared occasional visits. I always knew he would be there for me if I needed him. The relationship between a brother and sister transcends time and distance. Even though he was far away, K.W. was still my protector and defender.

Our lives moved in different directions as we got older. With families and job responsibilities consuming most of our energy, we saw each other less often, except for holidays and special events. I chose a somewhat sim-plistic lifestyle, whereas he became a successful doctor before entering the political side of health care. In light of the bumpy childhood we had endured, I was especially proud of his many accomplishments. K.W. was on the go constantly, traveling the globe for his job, but I still knew I could count on him to be my protector and defender in time of need. And more than once I called on him to do just that. Each time, no matter where he was, he would do whatever was necessary to help me. *But what could I ever do to help him?* That question surfaced often in my mind. There seemed to be nothing he really needed. Nothing, that is, except a healthy wife.

When I learned that my sister-in-law, a diabetic since her teens, was on dialysis and needed a kidney transplant, I realized there was something special I could do for my brother in an indirect way.

"K.W., I'd like to test to be your wife's kidney donor," I offered.

He was touched by my offer, but reminded me that she and I weren't related. "There's not much of a likelihood that you two will even match."

But I was adamant about testing. "We'll never know unless we try," I insisted. "And if by chance we do match, I'm more than willing to do this for her—and for you."

Surprisingly, we did match quite well. After months of further testing to ensure that I was perfectly healthy, my brother was still ready to allow me a graceful way to with-draw my offer.

"You really don't have to do this, you know. I'm honored that you would even offer," he said.

"I'm not backing out now," I assured him.

Less than a year after our initial cross-match test, K.W.'s wife and I were given a surgery date. We needed to be at the hospital by 5:00 AM on the day of our scheduled surgery. I would be wheeled into the operating room first so that my healthy left kidney could be removed. Shortly after that, my sister-in-law would be placed in the room across the hall where doctors would place my kidney in her abdomen. Both of our families came to lend their support, and since it would be a long day for everyone, they all dressed in casual, comfortable clothes—all except my brother. He wore a three-piece business suit.

"Dad," my niece inquired, "why are you so dressed up when we're going to spend all day sitting in this waiting room?"

He was quick with his answer. "Because if anything happens to go wrong, they'll listen to someone in a three-piece suit."

We all laughed, but I was deeply touched that just as it had always been, my brother was there to be my protector and defender should the need arise. Fortunately, the surgeries went smoothly and afterward, K.W. dutifully divided his attention between his wife and me.

The new kidney restored my sister-in-law to a state of health she had not known in years, giving my brother back the healthy wife he had once had. We know there are no promises for her future health, but I can make one prediction with confidence: K.W. will continue to be my protector and defender. Despite the uncertainty of life, some things just never change.

Caroleah Johnson

Remember When?

We do not know the true value of our moments until they have undergone the test of memory.

                                        Georges Duhamel

My younger brother Brent and I were only fourteen months apart. We were close growing up and very good friends. So it was hard when we started high school and he chose a different path. It was hard not having him as a friend anymore.

I married young and moved to Washington, leaving California and my childhood behind. My family was worried about me, saying I would "live in poverty." But Brent never said that. He came to visit my husband and me for our first Thanksgiving. He was our first real guest and laughed about us only having two chairs around our kitchen table.

"Hey, there's normally only the two of us," I told him.

We hadn't seen the need to buy extras when we purchased the table and chairs. After all, we weren't exactly in a position to afford the luxury of empty chairs. Besides, we could borrow chairs from the guy who lived in the apartment across from us.

"And can we borrow a big knife again, too?" I asked our neighbor when he handed me a borrowed chair. "You know, for the turkey." The guy smiled and obliged.

My brother chuckled. "You don't have knives?"

"We have knives," I said. "Just not big ones." What we had were dinner knives. There wasn't a need for other fancy kinds. After all, we were living on hot dogs and macaroni and cheese.

Over Thanksgiving dinner, we did what my brother and I always did when we got together. We started all of our conversations with "Remember when . . . ?"

"Remember when we spilled the entire bottle of shampoo on the bathroom floor and then ice-skated around in it for the whole day?" Brent asked.

"Yeah," I laughed. That had been the greatest day. "Until Dad caught us and gave us spankings for making such a horrible mess."

"Yeah," Brent raised his eyebrows. "It was a mess." It had taken us the rest of the day to clean it up. But Brent didn't dwell on that. Instead, he went on.

"Remember that time we planned to stay up all night?"

I laughed. "Yeah and you fell asleep even before our usual bedtime."

We went on and on with our "Remember whens . . . ," enjoying the same stories we told each and every time we got together. It was so good having my brother back, my friend, the only person who shared these childhood memories with me. It was wonderful.

When it was time for him to leave, I held him tight, not wanting him to go. But he was in college now, a whole life away from me.

"Remember, this Thanksgiving feast was your Christmas present from me," I told him for the hundredth time. We were broke; he was broke. And we hadn't given real gifts to each other in years.

When Christmas rolled around, a package came from Brent. I opened the box and bawled. It was a butcher's block with expensive, fancy knives.

Brent died not long after that. It's been almost twenty years now, but I still have those knives. I will have them forever and always. And someday, when I'm old and done with this world, I'll see my brother again, and I'll say, "Remember when . . . ?"

Melanie Marks

The Short and the Long of It

Change starts when someone sees the next step.

William Drayton

The empty appearance inside my house only increased the void in my heart from a miscarriage. Lying in my bed, I saw the outward signs of my recent move: boxes half unpacked, windows stark and untreated, nothing homey, nothing cozy, and worst of all, a bedroom wall color that would depress even the most ebullient occupant. *If only I had energy to cover it with a fresh coat of paint,* I said sadly to myself.

Something else aggravated the hurt in the pit of my stomach—the realization that I didn't have the strength to attend the long-anticipated reunion with my only sibling, Dick, and his family. It meant a lot because I had been away in the Peace Corps for two years and hadn't seen him in such a long while.

I remembered in high school how I had looked forward to Dick coming home from college for the holidays. I had worn myself out decorating the house, baking cookies, and because of my excitement, losing sleep over it. When he finally walked through the door, I lay bedridden with the flu. *How sad it had been back then to hear the party going on downstairs without me. Now another party with Dick was again passing me by.*

Six years older than me, Dick had always rescued his little sister from the consequences of childhood inquisitiveness: swarming bees, a galloping horse, and a young alligator's jaws. As I became a more sedate teenager, he gave me my first compliment and my first dance, chaperoned my first party, and took me to my first fraternity open house. But those "rescues" and "firsts" soon became things of the past. I was now an adult with grown-up problems. I couldn't see how the brother of my youth could possibly help me anymore.

My thoughts turned to the current family gathering a few short miles away. I knew Dick and his wife and children were perching themselves on the high stools around Mom and Dad's breakfast bar. Mom would serve a half grapefruit followed by poached eggs on toast with a side of sausage, and finish up with homemade waffles and maple syrup. They would linger over their food until the kitchen was saturated with the rich aroma of coffee and chatter.

I shed a few tears on my pillow, feeling thoroughly worthless and left out, even though I had told my family I needed to rest.

Brothers are for childhood, I thought as I drifted in and out of a dream world about happier days gone by. I saw Dick and me romping with our furry collie puppies; Dick and me ice-skating in the backyard rink; Dick and me playing hide-and-seek on hot summer nights; and Dick and me jumping into big waves at Lake Michigan.

As I came out of my reverie, I was vaguely aware of repeated knocking on the door. I wearily put on my bathrobe and slippers, shuffled downstairs, turned the knob, and peeked through the crack. A halo of morning light formed around a tall, familiar figure.

Squinting, I said, "Is it you, Dick? How wonderful to see you!"

He returned my hug with a kiss. "Great to see you, sis. What a shame about your miscarriage."

Stunned by his unexpected arrival, I just smiled. He shifted the bulky equipment in his arms and explained, "At breakfast, I heard that you wanted to have your bedroom painted white. Since your hubby is busy at work, your painter has arrived!"

He came in with buckets clanging and brushes dangling. Focused entirely on helping me, he seemed again like that teenager of long ago who had worked so hard at a factory just to bless our family with the gift of our first sound system.

I followed him into my master bedroom where he covered the bed with a tarp and mixed the paint in the can. Too weary to socialize, I flopped down on a mattress in an adjacent room and caught comforting glimpses of him through the open door.

He removed hardware, taped molding, applied the primer, and finally the finish coat. Using precise movements and careful strokes, he wanted the job perfect for his sister. At the end of the day, he tiptoed out of the house, everything left neater than he found it, while I, the poorest of company, had fallen into a restful sleep.

When I awoke, not only had the master bedroom received a facelift, so had my spirits. Even my body felt less wounded and more restored. I marveled that Dick had rescued me again by his labor of love for me in my infirmity.

And then it hit me. He hadn't only been my brother for a few childhood years, but would be my brother for all my adult years, too. That was the short and the long of it, and how happy that realization made me feel.

Margaret Lang

Peas in a Pod

Around 4:00 AM I was awakened from a deep sleep, as if I had heard a dreadful noise. I glanced around recalling the unfamiliarity of the guest room where I was staying. My brow dripped with sweat, and I could feel a tiny pool of moisture at the small of my back. My stomach swam and my heart beat like a race car circling around the track at full speed. I picked up my cell phone, shifted through the contacts, and settled on one. The phone rang at the other end as I rocked my body back and forth to comfort myself.

"Hello," said a warm, male voice.

"It's me," I said, choking back the tears.

"Okay. I'm here. What's going on?"

"What if I made a mistake?" I was having a severe panic attack about a security deposit I had just made on an apartment.

"It's okay. If you end up not liking the apartment, you can always look for another one, right?"

"Right. But what if I made a horrible mistake?"

"You didn't at all. It's just a deposit. You'll have time to find another apartment if you need to."

I sobbed some more through the conversation until my breathing slowed, like a train easing to a stop on the tracks. When I finally calmed down, I hung up the phone and fell back asleep.

It wasn't the first or the last middle-of-the-night phone call that I made to my twin brother. I had fallen into a deep depression due to some unforeseeable life circumstances, and throughout my numerous panic attacks, he was there for me.

Growing up with a twin brother was special. I always felt unique in school as we shared the same teachers and friends. Birthdays were always joint celebrations, even if he was five minutes older than me. And I was never lonely for a playmate; we did everything together all the way through high school.

I remember wanting to be just like him athletically. We played the same sports, and I never backed down from neighborhood football or hockey games, especially since I was the only girl. I'd let him strap some goalie pads to my legs and shoot pucks at me in the driveway. Sometimes, after a fresh snow, we'd play football in the front yard just so we could tackle each other into a pile of white powder.

I excelled in English; he always excelled in math and science. Since we often had the same teacher, I would finish the English assignment and he would complete the math. Then we'd swap and copy each other's work. (I passed math with flying colors until college, when he wasn't there to help me through it.)

Many times at night, when I couldn't sleep, I would wander from my bedroom into his and climb into the top bunk. He slept on the bottom bunk. In the morning, he would wake up, see me there, and think nothing of it. I must have crawled into that top bunk at least a hundred times. I remember one night when he crawled into my bed. He had watched a show about aliens before he had gone to bed. It was the only time he ever admitted to being scared.

My twin brother and I are actually quite different. I paint with words, expressing myself through stories, poems, and novels. He dabbles in something more concrete, selling prescription drugs to doctors. He likes looking at what's in front of him and not going any deeper. Me, I like digging to the bottom of things. I like to let my emotions flow, whether painful or joyous. He's not very expressive and often keeps his emotions hidden; I wear my heart on my sleeve for the world to see.

I remember the first birthday we celebrated apart—how it felt like something (or someone) was missing. He called me to say, "Happy birthday and I love you." I think I almost cried. We've remained close throughout the years after high school and college. Somehow, as we've both gotten a little older, we've grown even closer. I have always known that I could count on him. But after recent events, I now know he'll be there for me through anything. Regardless of how different we may be, there is something that we will always have in common. We are brother and sister. We are twins. Even at four in the morning.

Lyndsey D'Arcangelo

"You've always been such a good listener, brother."

The Greater Gift

A candle loses nothing by lighting another candle.

Father James Keller, M.M.

What would you do differently if you could go back and do it over? I have many answers to this age-old question, including saying "yes" when Herbert Williams asked me to dance in fifth-grade gym class, rather than being so shy about the whole thing. It wasn't like he was asking me to marry him.

Another answer I'd give is I would have practiced my piano much more devotedly. Oh, how I wish I could play some of those old-time favorites now. The third thing is I would have used my time more effectively while in college. And I would have been a better friend.

But an answer I'm ashamed to admit is that I would have been a better big sister. I wasn't a total ogre, but I wasn't the greatest, either. I was a typical big sister, and David was a typical little brother. We loved each other but had a wonderful knack for getting on each other's nerves. I was five years older than him and way too cool to be wasting my time on little brothers.

When David would ask me to play catch with him, I would go out and play, but I'd usually end the game by yelling at him about how bad he was at throwing the ball. I would begrudgingly take him to movies. But I was sure to let him know that I was only taking him out of the sheer goodness of my heart—and he'd darn well better appreciate it.

I loved him, of course, so if I'd had a chance for a do-over, being a better sister to David would have been one of my wishes. And as life sometimes has a way of winding back around and presenting us with the most profound opportunities, I got my wish. I did get my chance to make it up to David and be a good big sister, but not in the way I would have hoped. According to David, I gave him a great gift. According to me, he gave me much more than I ever gave him.

David was forty-three when he called to tell me he had been diagnosed with non-Hodgkin's lymphoma. We were devastated, especially since it looked like the diagnosis had come too late. However, true to character, David put up a gallant fight and maintained a positive attitude. I was there with him when he got his first dose of chemotherapy. His illness would be an interesting and sometimes terrifying journey as we learned to traverse the heart-rending path of cancer treatment that involved clinics, clinical trials, doctors, nurses, and other cancer patients.

Near the end of his second year of fighting the disease, David's doctor told him that there wasn't any other treatment they could give him. The only tiny light of hope David's doctor could offer was a research project at Duke University that involved adult stem cells. David signed up for it. He had no other options left.

Family members sent off blood to see if any of us would

be a match to donate stem cells. Dad and I were both found to be matches. Dad volunteered immediately, donated his stem cells, and they were given to David. Two months later, I sat beside David when we got the dreadful news that Dad's stem cells had not "taken."

David had to make a decision about whether to go through another adult stem-cell treatment. Preparing to receive the stem cells involved a grueling procedure of being injected with major doses of chemo over the course of a week, in an effort to kill anything in the body that would attack the foreign stem cells. It wasn't easy to watch, so I know it couldn't have been easy to endure. David had already gone through it once and his body was much weakened. But again, my little brother had no other options, so it was my turn to help.

After the week of preparatory chemo and my donation of stem cells, David and I trudged across the dark and rainy street from the bone marrow clinic and checked into the hospital. David climbed up onto the bed and soon a nurse walked in with a bag of what looked like tomato soup. It was my stem cells. The nurse hung it from the IV tower and hooked it up to David's port. It was then I saw David reach up and wipe his eyes.

"This is it," he whispered. "This is my last chance." Then he took a breath and said, "As soon as this is over, we're going to go play catch."

It was then that I saw a little boy throwing a baseball to me. I saw him tagging along with me to the movies. I also saw a little boy who, no matter how mean I was to him, kept hanging around, with a big, toothy grin and a positive attitude, just glad to be with me. And then I started to remember times when we sat together and laughed about funny movies, and whispered together the night before Christmas, wondering what Santa Claus would bring us. I remembered him dancing with me at my wedding. I remembered listening to him play his guitar. And I knew that if I remembered the good parts, then so did David. Yes, I had given him my stem cells, but he had given me the even greater gift of realizing that I hadn't been such a horrible big sister after all.

I took his hand and told him that now the two of us—he and I, his cells and mine—would fight this thing together.

My stem cells took, but just barely, and our celebration was short-lived. David's cancer was too fierce and no amount of stem cells, at least at that point, could fight the battle. David died with his family and friends at his side.

I'll always be thankful that I was given the chance to be a better big sister, and to give David my stem cells. But I know the greater gift I gave him was love.

Megan Martin

Battle Strategies

He that always gives way to others will end in having no principles of his own.

Aesop

When we were children, one of my younger brother's prized possessions was a genuine Hopalong Cassidy pocketknife, complete with a textured plastic handle. A silver-colored image of the beloved cowboy astride his rearing horse was glued to the plastic. Billy managed to hold on to the knife for several months after the Christmas he received it, but, unfortunately, the following summer he lost it in the park beside our house. He was only nine, but he stoically took his scolding for being careless with his possessions.

One Sunday afternoon, our little sister, five-year-old Bonnie, who was determined to learn how to play "jacks," had somehow coerced Billy into playing the game with her on the broad front step at the front of our house. A boy about a year older and a lot bigger than Billy stopped his bicycle on the sidewalk and called to my brother.

"Hey, I just found a knife in the park."

"It's mine," Billy announced. He left Bonnie on the step

and walked over to the boy, who stood on the sidewalk with his bicycle balanced between his legs.

"How do you know it's yours?" he demanded.

"Because I lost mine over there," Billy gestured toward the park. Bonnie joined her brother. She looked from one to the other as the conversation progressed. From the living room window, my mother, dad, and I could hear the discussion quite well. Dad got up from the couch and stood beside the window where he could watch the situation unfold.

"That doesn't mean it's your knife," the boy stated. "When did you lose yours?"

"This summer. It's been awhile—sometime after school was out." Billy nonchalantly put his hands in his pockets. He was a negotiator. Bonnie, on the other hand, was a combatant. Both of them usually worked out confrontations to their own advantage, but Bonnie's approach was more direct and much quicker.

"Janie, come watch this," Dad said to my mother with a smile. Mom and I joined Dad at the window.

"Oh yeah?" the boy challenged. "What did your knife look like?"

"It's a Hopalong Cassidy knife with a silver picture on the side," Billy said. The boy looked at the sidewalk and shifted his bicycle.

"That don't mean nothin'," he countered. "What color is the handle?"

"Black. It has little ridges in it." Billy sounded very calm.

His adversary kept one hand on the handlebar of his bike and withdrew the knife in question from his pocket.

"That's my knife," Billy told him, after catching a glimpse of it.

"You can't prove it," the boy taunted. "You can't prove it's yours, and I'm gonna keep it." He started to put the knife back in his pocket.

"You give my brother back his knife!" Bonnie flew at the bigger boy with the fury of the just. She attacked him with both hands and pushed him, nearly toppling him onto the sidewalk. He dropped the knife and it clattered onto the pavement. He grabbed the bike's handlebars with both hands to keep from falling, while Bonnie continued to hit him with doubled fists. Billy picked up the knife.

"Keep the old knife!" the boy shouted, and Bonnie backed away from him. He found his balance and pedaled away.

"It's broke," Billy said. Bonnie stared at the knife in his hand, and then looked up at her big brother's face. She put her hands on her hips, stepped away from him, and glared after the enemy, who was already half a block away. "The silver piece came off when he dropped it, and the blade is all rusty," Billy continued.

"Maybe Daddy can fix it," Bonnie suggested.

Daddy, in the meantime, laughed quietly at the hot-headed little girl, who was so much like him. When my brother and sister came in to tell us about the triumphant outcome of the skirmish, Dad was appropriately sympathetic and proud. He led the way to his tool shop in the garage, where he restored the silver Hopalong Cassidy to its rightful place on the knife.

To this day, some fifty-five years later, our little sister, Bonnie, still comes rampaging to the rescue when any of her family is in trouble, while Billy, the calm one, surveys any given situation and would still rather negotiate.

Barbara Elliott Carpenter

Dance Lessons

Don't let life discourage you; everyone who got where he is had to begin where he was.

Richard L. Evans

My sister Anna was a good dancer. But not until I fell in love with a girl named Helen in English class back at Holy Family High School did I ever think of asking Anna to teach me.

Anna was twenty years old, and I was fifteen. We both shared a love of rock'n'roll, as did most young people back in 1957. Only the year before, Elvis had rocked the music world with "Heartbreak Hotel," and Little Richard was screaming out hits like "Ready Teddy," "Tutti Frutti," and "Long Tall Sally." They were songs that required knowledge of the current dances and an understanding of the workout rhythm of Little Richard's frenetic beat. On a Friday dance night, getting out on the high-school gym floor without this knowledge and understanding was tantamount to an admission of hopeless stupidity or an attempt to commit social suicide.

So I asked Anna to teach me how to do the simple slow

dance, the Montclair, and the complicated fast dance, the Lindy. She was a very good teacher. Anna and I listened to WINS Radio and I got in a lot of practice dancing, learning the steps she was patiently teaching me. It wasn't easy. After all, I was the guy who, up until falling in love with Helen, wanted nothing to do with dancing, or, for that matter, with falling in love. I dreaded getting up in front of all those people and making a dancing fool of myself.

"Don't be worried about all the other people at the dance," Anna had reassured me. "Most of them aren't watching you anyway, and those who are watching you are probably saying, 'Hey, he's a good dancer. Look at those moves!'"

Anna had a way about her. And she made learning to dance as simple as possible, but the steps were always difficult for me. I remember her telling me how much more important it was to dance with the beat than it was to know the steps. "If somebody knows all the steps, but is not dancing to the music, isn't that worse?" she asked me.

The two of us danced every day after school and then again after dinner, before I did my homework. Little by little it got easier and I felt more relaxed. I began to hear and feel the beat and my feet learned how to translate that beat into steps, albeit a little different than what others were dancing.

When the next Friday night dance finally came, you'd think I would have taken Helen, but I didn't. I went alone. This time, however, I did not take my usual position leaning against the back wall. I smiled a lot, waved at dancing classmates, softly sang the lyrics to the songs, and I walked around the perimeter of the dance floor in a rhythmic movement, like someone training for the big game.

Then I spotted "my" Helen, who had come to the dance with her girlfriends. Mustering up all my courage, I asked her to dance and she said "yes." We danced to "The Great

Pretender." Then we snuggled close to "Only You." When someone asked her to dance and she agreed, I figured maybe I wasn't as good a dancer as Anna told me I was, or perhaps I wasn't really in love after all. I asked another girl to dance.

It was a fun night. My sister had advised me not to take dancing too seriously. "Make mistakes," she'd said, "but keep dancing!" That's exactly what I did.

Just two Friday dance nights earlier, my friends and I had been pointing at the dancers, picking out the goofiest among them, and laughing at their paces. Now I was asking one girl after another to come out on the dance floor with me. The self-confidence I felt inside me traveled down to my dancing feet and it seemed I could do no wrong. "You're a great dancer," one girl said. I flashed her a thank-you smile, then whirled her around as Jerry Lee Lewis sang out "A Whole Lot a Shakin' Going On."

Months later, Anna married Ciro, a man who couldn't dance! At their wedding, I danced a few numbers with my sister, and I felt like a million dollars.

Thanks to Anna's dance lessons, I still get out there, particularly for the slow and fast dances of those "Fabulous '50s." My wife, Sharon, and I enjoy the dance floor, but had it not been for my dear sister Anna, I would still be sitting out all those dances or standing against a wall, keeping my jacket well pressed.

Salvatore Buttaci

Beyond Words

Stories can conquer fear, you know. They can make the heart bigger.

Ben Okri

When my brother was four years old, he became very ill with tonsillitis. He endured infection after infection and every complication one could possibly get. None of us blinked an eye at the dinner table when someone said, "Jamie's choking!" Mom would just help him out.

In the "olden days," a tonsillectomy was a rite-of-passage; most kids got their tonsils taken out. It was such a common procedure there seemed no reason for concern. I'd had mine removed when I was four. Now, at the ripe old age of seven, I assured my little brother that nothing bad could possibly happen. He would even get ice cream for dinner!

I told Jamie how I remembered rolling down the long hallway on my way to surgery, the elevator ride while perched on my hospital bed, the crisp smell of antiseptic, and the cool green tile walls on a never-ending tunnel that led to the operating room. I can still remember the nameless smiling face that covered my mouth and nose with a mask, which smelled as sweet as a meadow. Then my next memory was of family crowding around, loving me—and ice cream.

The day finally arrived when my brother would be free of his bothersome glands. I remembered my happy, mysterious memories and hugged him when his turn came to go into surgery. I knew he would be back soon with his own peaceful memories.

We waited in the hospital lounge. My mind was occupied with the books and toys that someone had graciously left for me to play with. I had no idea that it was taking too long. My parents tell us now that they knew something was wrong. But that day, they held their worry and fears tight to their hearts. Right there beside them and their dread, I was happy and unaware of the fact that my little brother was in trouble.

Finally, a doctor came out and explained that complications had arisen. After removing each of the glands, the flow of blood from a vessel close to the surface could not be stopped.

As an adult, I can imagine the frantic transition from a routine tonsillectomy to a desperate race to save a young child. The doctors and nurses worked hard to keep my little brother alive. He required two blood transfusions before they were able to stop the flow. That was quite a lot of blood to lose since Jamie only weighed thirty-five pounds.

After being stabilized, Jamie was wheeled into a hospital room. My parents were apprised of his condition, but we were not allowed to visit. He had not regained consciousness yet. By this time, I knew that something was not right. I was only seven, but I could feel the worry in my parents' hearts. The doctors told us they had done all they could; it was now up to Jamie and he had to fight to wake up.

We were left there to pray that my little brother had the strength to fight for his life. I thought, *did he know that we loved him so much? Did he know he had to wake up, that it wasn't just another Saturday morning? Could he feel our strength just outside his door?*

I wanted to go to my brother and shake him awake, just like I did at home. I couldn't understand why that wouldn't work. I pleaded with my mom and dad to let me try! *He was my brother; he would hear me,* my small mind reasoned. I suppose they must have spoken to a nurse, because soon afterward, somebody explained to me it would be okay to quietly read my brother a story. Being newly literate, I glowed at the chance to prove my reading skills to anyone who would listen. They made me a snuggly spot beside my brother on his bed. He was so small and still, I had to be careful.

I remember cracking the storybook. I remember quietly stumbling over the unfamiliar words. I read for a while. I also remember looking up at my parents to see tears sliding down their cheeks—tears streaming down my big, strong daddy's face. I wondered what I could have done so wrong that would make him cry? *Had I read too loud? Had I been trouble?* I turned and looked at my brother. He was awake and quietly listening to the story I was telling. He had awoken to the sound of my voice.

The next thing I knew I was telling him he could ask for ice cream! I remember they brought him some green ice cream. Jamie just shook his head; he didn't like green ice cream. They found him some Jell-O instead. Mom helped Jamie get a little of the cold liquid down his throat while my dad gave me a big hug. Guess who got the ice cream!

Donna Dawkin

$\overline{6}$

THROUGH
OUR EYES

*Perception is merely reality filtered through
the prism of your soul.*

Christopher A. Ray

Yeah Me!

To praise is an investment in happiness.

George M. Adams

It was "Grandma Day" with our son's children—
Caitlyn, Brandon, and Jordyn—and Brandon's turn to pick
a game to play. He chose the Hippo game. For those of
you who are unfamiliar with this particular game, it has a
board with four opposing hippos, each facing the center of
the board, ready to gobble up marbles as the player skillfully operates his or her plunger. I say skillfully, because as
we were playing, Brandon showed the most aptitude for
the game; his sisters and I were painfully lagging behind.

The game was extremely sturdy and well built. I say
this because Brandon's "skill" consisted of vigorously and
rapidly plunging his gobbling button, a technique that,
according to Las Vegas odds, guaranteed that the more
frequently he opened and closed his hippo's mouth, the
more marbles he gobbled up.

The game progressed until Brandon's hippo had gulped
down the last of the marbles. We counted carefully and—
voila!—Brandon was declared the winner.

He raised his small fists in self-acclaim, rose up in a victory dance, and shouted, "Yeah me! Yeah me!"

Brandon's playing skill continued, producing the exact same results game after game. "Yeah me! Yeah me!" he shouted each time, dancing up a storm.

As the good, observing grandmother, I quietly watched the progress of Brandon's victory celebrations, thinking to myself, *this kid really loves winning, for sure, but how will he handle defeat?*

My answer came with the next hippo-round. Brandon slammed his control and his hippo devoured marble after marble—until the tide turned and Caitlyn began pegging marbles in quick succession. *Ah-ha,* I thought, *now we will see how Brandon loses.*

My eyes bugged out and my mouth dropped open as I watched in astounded pleasure. My loving grandson raised his fists and jumped up in a victory dance for his sister, declaring, "Yeah you! Yeah you! Yeah you!"

My eyes misted, I swallowed the lump in my throat, and my grandmother's heart burst with pride. I knew my grandson would be a great brother.

Paulie Tietz

Poor Boy

When you're the youngest sibling in a large family, people pity you.

"You'll wear hand-me-downs the rest of your life," they warn. Or, "Your parents will be confined to wheelchairs by the time you graduate from high school."

But when you're the youngest *and* the only boy, there's no end to the empathy:

"Poor boy. His sisters will never leave him alone." Or, "Only boy in a family of six? He'll be lucky if he ever gets a date!" Or, "Have his sisters dressed him in a skirt yet?"

The day after our son, Andrew, was born, Grandma lugged our five little girls to the hospital to meet their new brother. Reverently, the girls shuffled into the birthing room like ducklings out of water. The girls didn't know what to expect. They had seen little boys before, but to have a real live brother in their own family was a curiosity!

"Will it bite?" whispered the two-year-old.

"Of course not. Babies don't even have teeth," piped in the seven-year-old. "I hear that little brothers have other parts, though, that sisters don't have. Right, Mom?"

"Here we go," mumbled my husband, Dave, under his breath.

"What kind of parts?" chimed in the five-year-old, as she scrambled up on the bed with the baby and me. She began poking at his little blankets. "Like an extra stomach? I read that cows have two stomachs."

My two oldest daughters shot looks across the room. "Mom, tell them to stop."

Just then, an efficient-looking nurse hurried into the room. She surveyed our crowded quarters. "Oh, friends and neighbors shouldn't be in here now," she advised.

"These are my children, Andrew's sisters," I responded.

"Poor boy!" she threw out hastily as she yanked my boy from my grip, plopped him on the bed, and unwrapped him from his security blanket like a leftover sandwich. "I'm just going to check his circumcision and see if everything's healing well."

Before I could intervene (after all, I wasn't actually the Goddess of Speed twenty-four hours after giving birth), the nurse casually opened Andrew's tiny diaper before a live audience of five wide-eyed girls.

The sisters stared. In stereo. Their faces shriveled up as though the nurse had pulled a moldy sandwich from a refrigerator.

"Eeeeewwwwww!" they gasped, in stereo again.

"Is that what makes him a brother?" asked one of the girls. I didn't know which one. I had squeezed my eyes shut to pray, "Dear God, help me . . . "

"It's yucky!" shrieked the two-year-old.

Even my older daughters were appalled. "There's so much . . . flesh."

"Will it fall off later like his belly button?" That was the seven-year-old again.

Poor boy. What have I done? I tormented myself. *This little innocent male is destined to remain an oddity in his own family. He'll grow up with a confused male identity and it will be my fault for conceiving him!*

My husband stepped closer to me. He must have read my mind, and his warm embrace calmed my fears. "It's alright, honey. Someday he'll be thankful he has so many sisters."

"I hope you're right," was all my mind could muster.

About two years later, Andrew was in the throes of toddlerdom. He could run. He could say, "No!" He could say, "jackhammer" and "truck" and even "ice cream." But despite the girls' best efforts, he didn't say his sisters' names. They felt hurt that he could name a power tool before he could say any of their names.

One fall day while playing outside, Andrew fell hard. He wailed like a fire engine and couldn't put his weight on his left leg. "Broken?" my husband suggested.

We called our neighbor to care for the girls, strapped Andrew in his car seat, and rushed to the hospital. Five little girls huddled together in the front yard, crying and waving like their brother was going off to war. All the way to the hospital, Andrew writhed and bawled. Nothing would console him, not a bottle, a blankie, or a story.

Once in the emergency room, physicians examined him while Dave and I held our baby on the table, kissing his wet little cheeks. It was so much pain for a baby and no one could take the pain away.

Then, between crying jags, our twenty-month-old began saying, over and over, "Caca . . . Han . . . Em . . . SaSa . . . Yidee!"

The nurse finally turned to me. "What's he saying?" she asked loudly over Andrew's pleas.

"I think . . . I think he's calling for his sisters!" my husband marveled. Dave and I looked at each other then tears streamed down our faces.

"Andrew, do you want Cassie, Hannah, Emma, Sarah, and Lydia?" Dave asked his boy.

"Okay," Andrew responded.

After Andrew was splinted and medicated, we drove him home. Pulling in the driveway, we spotted one . . . two . . . three . . . four . . . five little girls running toward the car. Andrew's crying ceased. "Caca . . . Han . . . Em . . . SaSa . . . Yidee!" he yelled, kicking his cracked leg up and down with excitement.

Five sisters hugged that boy. And kissed him. And coddled him. But his oldest sister summed it up best. Scooping up her broken little brother, she reassured him, "We're here, Andrew. We're here. We're your sisters, and we'll always be here for you."

Poor boy.

Cristy Trandahl

Delivery Room Surprise

Our brightest blazes of gladness are commonly kindled by unexpected sparks.

Samuel Johnson

Heading to the hospital at three in the morning, I could feel my stomach tightening, the pain in my back getting worse. My husband, Rob, flew down the freeway, and I knew that this hot, muggy night in July was the night my twin girls would be born.

For almost nine months I had prepared for this very moment. Growing up, I had always wanted a sister for myself. When the ultrasound technician had told me almost six months earlier that I was having twin girls, who were probably identical, I was thrilled by the news. Now I could give my children the gift of the sisterly bond I had so wanted in my own life as a child who only had a brother. Over the months, as my pregnancy progressed, my husband and I began envisioning our future with two daughters. We named them Samantha and Sydney and eagerly anticipated the busy years to come.

As a first-time mother I was excited, of course. But I

would be lying if I didn't admit to being a bit sad that I wasn't having a little boy as well. I had grown up with an older brother, and when I pictured my ideal family, my picture contained both a boy and a girl. I had always dreamt of having a boy, a brother who would take care of his little sister, defending her from schoolyard bullies one minute, while teasing her about her ponytails the next. A little girl who would screen her brother's girlfriends and help him with his clothing choices as teenagers. I wished for my hypothetical children the brother-sister relationship that I had enjoyed growing up.

But my dream for the brother-sister relationship died when the ultrasound technician informed Rob and me that we would be having twin girls. We knew that we only wanted two children, so there would probably not be any more after this pregnancy. I grieved for my unborn girls, who would never have a brother they could torment with unsolicited makeovers and pajama parties full of giggling eight-year-olds.

On July 23, 2002, my labor progressed rapidly, and it wasn't long before Rob and I were in the delivery room preparing to meet Samantha and Sydney for the first time. After some trial and a little bit of drama, "Baby A" came into the world kicking and screaming. My obstetrician held up our new baby for me to see and announced, "Congratulations! It's a *boy!*"

"No," I protested. This was my first-born girl, this baby was supposed to be Samantha. Everyone knew I was having twin girls; the doctor must have been trying to be funny.

"No," I informed him again, making it clear that I was not in the mood for a joke. "No. It's not."

He held up the baby again, this time turning the squirming newborn toward himself. He took a closer look and smiled.

"Nope." He could barely contain his laughter. "I'm pretty sure that this is a boy. Congratulations, you have a son."

A boy? A boy! What was going on here? I was having twin girls!

It's hard to explain what I was feeling that night. I was confused and excited all at the same time. But I didn't have too long to ponder the situation because it wasn't too long before "Baby B" decided to make her appearance as well.

My baby girl was born twenty minutes later and our family was complete. When I finally held both of my healthy babies in my arms together for the first time, I gazed from my son to my daughter with wonder. In a matter of minutes, my future had changed, and with it, my hopes and dreams for our children. Now I held in my arms the beginning of a brand new brother-sister relationship.

Elena Aitken

You're Too Cute to Be a Boy!

As an only child, I often wished I had a brother or a sister. I envied friends who came from bigger families. I sometimes felt deprived and decided if I ever got married, I would have more than one child. After I did marry I was soon the young mother of two boys, only eleven months apart. When Joey was four and Greg was three, I was elated to learn we were expecting a third child.

"I'm praying and hoping this baby will be a little sister that you guys can be big brothers to," I told the boys one day, as my pregnancy became more obvious.

One night, just before I tucked him in, Greg decided to help me in my petition for a girl. "God, Mom really wants a girl. Could you make sure that it is a girl? And I think it would be nice to have a sister. I hope you're listening, God," he prayed.

"I think a sister would be nice, too, God," Joey piped up from his corner of the room. "Besides, if it's another boy, this bedroom will get too crowded," he added.

I smiled as I tucked them in and kissed them good night.

"Actually, another little brother would be a blessing, too," I added, just before turning off the lights.

Andrea was born July 31, 1963, and she was an adorable little girl from day one. Her father and I were elated. Her big brothers stared at her with wonder and became her protectors from the day they first saw her. And as she grew, her big brothers were her idols, as were her three boy cousins. She wanted to be like them, dress like them, and play with Tonka trucks and Hot Wheels and any other boy-toys they played with. Her own toys remained untouched. Dolls were looked at with disdain, and she resisted wearing the cute dresses I bought her in favor of pants and T-shirts. Clearly, the cute little blond daughter I had prayed for was a big-time tomboy, through and through.

When she was three, I was determined my little tomboy was going to wear the cute Easter outfit and bonnet I had gotten her for Easter services. Her brothers, six and seven by this time, had handsome Easter suits to wear.

"I don't want to wear a dress and a bonnet," Andrea cried, as I dressed her for church. "I want to wear a suit like Joey and Greg are wearing."

"You're a little girl and will dress like a little girl for church," I said to my tearful, angelic-looking tomboy.

"Well, when I grow up, then I'll be a boy," she retorted, tears rolling down her cheeks.

In the car on the way to church, Greg told Andrea, "God made you a girl, and it's too late to change his mind now, so you might as well get used to it."

"Yeah," Joey piped in. "Besides, you're too cute to be a boy. And we like you being a girl."

She smiled at Greg and Joey through her tears and stopped crying for a change. Her big brothers liked her being a girl!

Soon after that, I enrolled Andrea in dance school where she met other cute little girls. And at her very first recital, when she danced to "Alley Cat" and received a big hand and loud cheers from her brothers, who sat with us in the front row, her pride in being a girl was finally well established.

These days, Andrea is mom to two beautiful girls and still the cherished sister of two big brothers, whose brotherly devotion is as strong as ever.

Renie Burghardt

Chickabudee Berries

What guides us is children's responses, their joy
in learning to dance, to sing, to live together. It
should be a guide to the whole world.

Yehudi Menuhin

My children were playing outside together, as they did
nearly every day. I watched them from the swaying hammock with the baby nestled comfortably on my lap. Ellie
and Benjamin ran off to the sandbox, their words floating
back to me on the breeze. "We need to finish our mud
mountain!" Ellie shouted and I nodded as though I knew
what she was talking about. Finish implies started, and
they had not told me they were making a mud mountain.

They were beginning to keep secrets from me, secrets
between a brother and a sister. I couldn't see them—a
large pine tree stood between us—but I could hear the
chatter of their voices, the occasional rise of a squabble
and the murmur of negotiation. I saw colorful movements
near the garden as they picked peaches from the ground
to decorate the mud mountain's summit.

The air was getting colder and my hands were turning

red. I knew that soon my children would complain about the cold and want to head indoors, but they were in childhood bliss.

"Let's pick chickabudee berries for the birds!" Ellie yelled, and her brother ran over with a cracked red pail. I watched as they carefully picked each red berry from an overgrown bush by our back porch. They dropped the bright red orbs into the pail and hunted through the green leaves for more. "Pick lots of berries, Benjamin," Ellie commanded. "The birds need food for the winter."

Benjamin's hands swept through the foliage, searching for missed berries. The sun dropped lower in the sky, and a cold wind blew Ellie's hair into her eyes as she talked to me, to her brother, but mostly to herself. "We need to harvest these berries before the winter comes. The birds will need food for the long cold winter."

"Yeah, the long cold winter is coming," Benjamin echoed.

The hammock creaked and brushed against leafless branches. The baby was falling asleep in my arms and I needed to start dinner. But I knew that if I moved from this spot, the spell would be broken and Ellie would complain of the cold and Benjamin would say he wanted to go inside, and the pail of berries would be forgotten on the cold ground and the birds would not have them for winter. So, I didn't move. I sat and I watched my children gather the berries, knowing this time was sacred, that this was one of childhood's finest hours.

When the berries were sufficiently gathered, brother and sister ran off to the edge of the woods, their shadows slanted away across the trampled grass. They flung the cracked red pail in the air and red chickabudee berries flew out, landing in the decaying leaves. I didn't tell them that the birds preferred the berries left on the branches, if the birds ate them at all. This moment was magic and could not be disturbed by practicalities.

"We picked chickabudee berries to help the birds!" Ellie exclaimed, running over to the hammock, and Benjamin nodded wisely. We headed indoors to the warm house, the spell broken, the magic temporarily at a halt. It would return tomorrow, when my children donned their coats to re-enter the private world that, as siblings, they had come to share. As we climbed the porch steps, I saw a few missed chickabudee berries among the glistening leaves.

Kimberly Misra

Until She's Two

We are all like one-winged angels. It's only when
we help each other that we can fly.

Luciano deCrescenzo

"I will love her until she's two," our six-year-old Jed said about his newborn sister.

Upon inspecting her for several minutes at a safe distance, Jed decided he would accept her, but he also let us know the limits we could expect. "She's a baby until she's two." The conclusiveness of his tone established that this was enough explanation for his decision.

We had worried a great deal about Jed's reaction to Kamryn's impending arrival. We had spoken to the other children about the baby, with mixed reactions. Nine-year-old Sydni was done being the only girl, eight-year-old Xavier established very specific parameters for his acceptance of the newborn, and three-year-old Quinn was ready to move up in the pecking order. Our work in preparing our family for Kamryn's arrival was not confined to Jed nor was it entirely successful, but in him, we faced a unique challenge.

Like most children with autism, Jed does not deal well with change. He also does not attach himself to people easily. Jed is logical and precise, and on more than one occasion my husband has accused me of watching too many Star Trek episodes during my pregnancy. I have occasionally regretted not naming our frustratingly precise son "Spock" when he has snippily disagreed with me: "It is not 4:30. It's 4:28."

Yet, we do not take for granted the miracle that Jed is able to attach to people at all. In fact, despite some severe, occasionally debilitating, symptoms, Jed's diagnosis places him "along the autism spectrum," but does not classify him as suffering from classic autism because he does form rare, but genuine, attachments. After meeting many parents of children with autism, our gratitude for his ability to do so is limitless.

We knew that integrating Kamryn into our routine would be a challenge. Jed is phenomenally stubborn, so he almost invariably wins fights that require stamina. We have tried to convince the other children that they do not need to capitulate to Jed's capacity for loud and prolonged screaming, but even I have to admit to giving in more often than I should despite a determination not to do so. In contrast, from the start, Kamryn faced off with him in a way that the rest of us could not. Of course, her own lung capacity established her prominence in the house almost immediately.

Miraculously, this boy, who is almost incapable of empathy and understanding emotions, learned that babies have little impulse control. He thought it was hilarious when she punched him with her tiny flailing fists, and, more often than ever before, his rare laughter would bubble uncontrollably from him. To see and hear my very serious child enjoy anything in this way has always provided needed balm to my ever-present anxiety about my challenged son.

Within a month of birth, Kamryn went to show-and-tell with Jed. Not surprisingly, he did not make eye contact with his fellow students or with me as he spoke about her, and his words were brief and virtually incomprehensible. But, as I stood beside him and held his sister in my arms, Jed's eyes focused steadily on Kamryn, drawing strength from her presence.

If there were an opposite disorder to autism, Kamryn would receive an unqualified diagnosis. As she has grown, she has become social to the extreme, believing that everyone wants to talk to her and giving each person an opportunity to do so, and to do so indefinitely. She is at the age where she loves the world, and her brothers and sister receive a great deal of affection. There is a strong and peculiar attachment between her and Jed, though. When we drop Jed off at school, she does her best drama-queen fake cry and sobs, "No more Jeddy for us." When she perceives that one of her siblings is picking on her brother, she fearlessly intervenes, screaming at the offender: "No! Don't be mean to Jeddy!" Of course, her anointed status as "master of the house" helps her do this with impunity.

As Kamryn tries to protect him, Jed tries to guide her. He often informs me of my shortcomings in caring for her in the monotone characteristic of his speech. "Kamryn needs new shoes. Those are getting too small." He pleads her case for her. "Kamryn's really hungry, and all that we have for her to eat are the cookies you told her she can't have." He also explains the facts of life to her. Upon her inaccurate declaration that she was a "big sister," Jed instructed, "You can't be a big sister until Mommy and Daddy decide to reproduce." Sometimes, his social shortcomings limit his helpfulness. Dora the Explorer, Kamryn's idol, always wears a seatbelt "so we can be safe!" (Dora also always speaks in exclamation points.) So, when Kamryn refuses to ride in her car seat, her siblings explain that Dora always wears a seatbelt for safety. Jed, however, is not as skillful with this encouragement. "Wear your seatbelt, or Dora will die," is clearly not the ideal way to promote seatbelt use.

Next month, Kamryn will be three—one year past Jed's non-negotiable, two-years-old deadline. Yet when we brought her to Jed's parent-teacher conferences last month, his teacher remarked that she had never seen Jed so animated as when Kamryn walked into the room. I admit that my maternal pride suffered a slight bruise, as I had walked into Jed's classroom numerous times and never elicited that response. Yet, watching Jed's smile and feeling the barely-repressed laughter start bubbling in him even as he maintained his characteristic downward gaze, I could not deny that he is different when she is around. More than anyone I know, Jed says what he means and means what he says, so I am reluctant to remind him of his pronouncement regarding the self-imposed limits on his love. Rather, I am simply relieved that this aspect of his relationship with his sister is as atypical as so many of the other aspects of it.

Laurie Heron

"Ignore my kid brother... his operating system is buggy."

Upgrades

*We cannot hold a torch to light another's path
without brightening our own.*

Ben Sweetland

As young children, they were best friends. My son,
Erick, was two and a half years older than my daughter,
LeeAnne. She idolized her big brother and tried to keep up
with him in every way. She cried when he started kindergarten. Erick in turn looked out for his little sister when
she started school. They played together, usually with
cars and GI Joes, but occasionally Barbie would join in.

But when junior high and high school set in, adolescence and sibling rivalry deteriorated their once close relationship. Erick would drive them to high school, but made
sure she left the car before he did. They hardly acknowledged each other's existence, even though they were in
some of the same activities. They barely got along.

Once LeeAnne was in college, things began to change.
Maybe it helped that they were at different universities.
Both had matured and the rivalry was less intense. At home
on college breaks, they laughed and played together again,

whether it was video games or playing catch in the back-yard. Slowly they were coming back together as friends.

College graduation came, and Erick moved out of state to begin his career. This was sad for all of us, especially LeeAnne.

A year later, we all anticipated LeeAnne's college graduation. In a conversation about this one day, Erick brought up the subject of a graduation gift for LeeAnne. My husband Rick and I had thought of upgrading some features on her car, since it was pretty basic and several years old. Erick had a different idea. He knew she would be going out of state to graduate school and wanted her to have a reliable car. His suggestion was to upgrade the gift to a *new* car for graduation. We couldn't believe our ears. This older brother who barely acknowledged her existence in high school wanted to surprise his little sister with a new car at college graduation!

Once we got past being quite shocked at the suggestion, we agreed to participate in the purchase and the "scheme." Rick would find the right car, and we would drive it to graduation.

During the next few weeks, Rick secretly test-drove cars. The scheme was masterfully hidden from her until the big day.

After the ceremony, LeeAnne and her roommates hosted a cookout. The time came for gifts to be opened. Erick sat next to LeeAnne on the sofa and handed her a heavy, medium-sized box. She was confident it was a new auto CD system.

LeeAnne was stunned when she pulled a clunky radio with big push buttons out of the box. In his unique style, and to play out the scheme, Erick had wrapped an old AM car radio in a car stereo box. She didn't quite know what to think or say about the old-fashioned radio. Where was the CD system?

She blurted, "Erick, your gift sucks!" and laughed, all at the same time.

The scheming brother played along, looking dejected and crushed.

Then Erick quietly spoke. "Keep looking."

She dug into the bottom of the box and found keys attached to a cardboard egg carton.

"Why did you give me keys to your car?" she asked with a confused look. (He had recently gotten one).

"They're not; they're keys to *your* car," was his calm but excited response. A short silence was followed by great joy.

"Gotcha!" Erick said with a sneaky smile and a hug.

Screams of, "LeeAnne's brother got her a car!" and, "I wish I had a brother like that!" were heard throughout the house.

Speechless and teary-eyed, LeeAnne walked outside with Erick to find out which car fit the key. She found the right one—a red Lancer that was fully equipped with a CD stereo system!

Our family will never forget that day. The scheme was pulled off, and LeeAnne fell for it. The memory of that day will remain in my heart. I realized that the upgrade didn't happen only with the gift, but within their relationship. This brother and sister were once again special to each other. And he even let her drive him home after graduation.

Nancy Kay Grace

Stinky Little Brothers

As I gazed into the eyes of my two-year-old Julia, holding her hands in mine, I shared the news she was getting a baby brother. Immediate joy overwhelmed Julia, as she was in complete favor of the wonderful surprise. "Hooray!" she shouted and danced circles of delight on the living room rug.

Why, it was positively the best present her heart could have imagined. In fact, she was ready to drop what she was doing immediately to go to the store and pick the baby out! Instead, she had to wait nine months before her adopted baby brother, Jay, would arrive from Guatemala. While Kevin and I completed mounds of paperwork to prepare for Jay's arrival, Julia did her part by relinquishing her pacifiers and tackling potty training; she wanted to give her baby brother her "passies" and diapers, the finest expression of love from a two-year-old big sister.

From the moment he arrived in our home, it was love at first sight between Julia and Jay. Though Julia quickly surmised that Jay was noisy, and he really knew how to stink up the house upon occasion, the two siblings were inseparable. However, when only two months later we learned the shocking news that Julia would receive *another* baby sibling, this time from her mother's womb, Julia had some very definite ideas about how this new baby would fit into the family picture.

Julia ordered, "This time, I want a baby sister!" I tried to explain that it was fine to want a baby sister, but only God could make that decision. She stuck her hands on her hips, "Well, God *knows* I already have a baby brother!"

A mother can only do so much to persuade a preschooler, and Julia was not budging from her demand for a sister. The day arrived for the ultrasound appointment. Julia went to preschool while I visited the doctor, and I was delighted to see a beautiful, healthy baby boy on the ultrasound monitor. But my joy was reduced somewhat as I realized that I was going to have to break the "bad news" to Julia.

After school, Julia immediately wanted to know if we were decorating the nursery pink or blue. When the answer was "blue," Julia didn't cry, but the disappointment reached deep down into her soul and settled. She sat in the back seat, head hanging low, eyes expressing her overwhelming loss of the dream of afternoons spent pouring pretend tea and playing house.

I had never seen anything hurt her heart so profoundly. I had to make her believe that a brother was truly God's very best gift for her. I explained from the front seat, "Julia, God is always watching our family, and God has noticed what a wonderful big sister you have been to Jay, so loving and kind, and how you are teaching him many things. And God has another baby boy that needs a family, so He decided to give you another baby brother."

Julia fell silent, pondering my words as she stared out the car window. I hadn't given it much thought, but as I said those words to Julia, I felt certain they were true. But would Julia believe that a second brother could be as delightful as a sister? Finally Julia broke her silence, revealing her deepest thoughts: "Momma, if I start being a mean big sister to Jay, do you think God will give us a girl?"

Now that John Mark, baby number three, has arrived, and Julia has found the capacity in her heart to love another brother after all, I marvel at the beauty of the innocence of childhood love between a sister and her brothers. Jay dutifully plays house with Julia and rocks baby dolls to sleep, completely decked out in fine princess gowns and frumpy hats. And then there are the moments when Julia humbles herself to play trucks on the kitchen floor, having more fun making her brothers giggle than from pushing a plastic truck while crawling on all fours.

How does it happen? What is the ingredient of the heart that makes a little girl with two baby brothers, the two people in the world who invaded her home and stole time and attention away from her mother and daddy, fall deeply in love with the culprits who break her toys and stink up the house with foul diapers? It must be love. It's the love that makes her eyes sparkle with the most supreme level of delight when she tag-teams with Jay to wrestle their daddy to the floor, or when she stretches forth her petite arms to cuddle baby John Mark on the couch. It's a love that thrives on togetherness, that unifies five people to live as one, and that makes belonging a privilege uniquely extended only to mommies and daddies, big sisters, and yes, even stinky little brothers.

Kimberly Sowell

$\overline{7}$

GOLDEN TIMES

*He who has done his best for his own time
has lived for all times.*

Friedrich von Schiller

Easter Bloomers

We are made to persist. That's how we find out who we are.

Tobias Wolff

On my sixth birthday during the summer of 1943, Mama confided to my older sister Patti and me that there was a baby on the way. Despite Grandpa's teasing that I'd soon have a baby sister, I had faith; I knew it would be a boy. I fully intended to remain the official "youngest daughter" for life, though I was perfectly willing to play the dual role of big sister.

When Joel was born on September 30, I was not surprised. But when he arrived home from the hospital, I was somewhat disappointed. As a new first grader, my favorite activity was playing school. I had been counting on this new family addition to join my dolls and me in my makeshift schoolroom. Baby Joel couldn't even sit up, let alone hold a pencil in his tiny fist. Mama comforted me, though, by painting a rosy picture of the future when Joel indeed would become my attentive pupil.

I bided my time, helping bathe and diaper him, joining

Mama in singing "Tura-Lura-Lural" to him at bedtime, admiring him when he finally could eat a peanut butter sandwich by himself. I waited for him to walk. I waited for him to talk. Finally, at the age of three, he began to join in play-school sessions.

But sometimes Joel didn't seem to take his lessons seriously, so as his teacher, I would inform him sternly that while the dolls were earning As, he'd be lucky to get a C. "It's C—A—T," I would pronounce, pushing back my bangs in exasperation.

"T—A—C," Joel would spell back, and then giggle and clap his hands. "Better than the dolls, huh?" I would throw up my hands in disgust.

Joel was equally cheerful in his Sunday school class, and talented as well, particularly excelling at coloring Bible story pictures. Then one Sunday as Easter neared, I overheard his teacher telling Mama that Joel would have the first line to recite in the group's recitation of a holiday poem. His opening line would be, "Easter lilies blooming remind us of the day." The other preschoolers would, in turn, complete the additional three lines of the quatrain.

At dinner that night I confided my fear that Joel wouldn't get the line straight. That's when Grandpa promised to help coach him, which immediately alarmed me. That perennial tease of a grandfather recently had turned his attentions to my innocent brother. He had told Joel that spaghetti was made from the worms that inhabited the garden. Joel no longer ate pasta. Another fib he told him was that grizzly bears roamed the hills above our home and feasted on wild blackberries. Joel no longer helped pick berries. But this was serious. I heard Grandpa assuring Joel that the first line of the poem was "Easter *bloomers* waving remind us of the day."

Determined that Joel would not disgrace the family by garbling his line, I set up a counterattack. As soon as I memorized my own Easter poem for the service, I began drilling Joel. "It's Easter lilies *blooming* remind us of the day," I would insist. Sometimes he would get it straight and sometimes he would repeat Grandpa's version. I decided to call upon divine reinforcement. "Remember," I threatened, "If you don't get this right, Jesus will be disappointed."

When we awoke that Easter morning, our baskets were already at the foot of our beds. I savored the sweet, chewy, yellow marshmallow Peep chicks first. As I got dressed, I downed a rainbow-hued hard-boiled egg, chewed a stick or two of Wrigley's Juicy Fruit, and gazed several times into the innards of my chocolate diorama egg. I counted my jellybeans and offered to trade Patti for the black ones, my favorites. From time to time, I would glance nervously at Joel, while Mama adjusted the collar of his sailor suit.

Then we went to church. Patti was the first of our family to perform, her alto soaring on a solo interval during the choir's rendition of "The Old Rugged Cross." I was next, reciting my poem, and then I took a seat in the front row to watch Joel's preschool class march onto the stage. The congregation chuckled as the toddlers jostled one another to get into line.

Finally, Joel stepped forward confidently. "Easter," he announced, and then paused. His eyes caught mine, and then flickered left towards Grandpa. "Easter," he began again. I held my breath. "Lilies," he enunciated clearly. "Blooming," he continued, "remind us of the day." He grinned his jack-o-lantern grin. I beamed back. The next child stepped forward.

Grandpa grumbled a bit on the way home, but I held Joel's hand and told him he would be getting an A on his next report card and a gold star, too. Then I leaned over and whispered that I knew that Jesus was pleased.

"Did I do better than the dolls?" he asked.

"Oh, yes," I said. "That's better than anybody in my class."

Even now Joel still chides me that I'm the overachiever, the "doer," the academic one in the family, always busy trying to teach, to mentor, to influence. That's certainly true. But what he overlooks is that as my first pupil, he indeed proved to be my teacher, teaching me the delights of watching somebody learn and succeed, teaching me to persist and persevere—and teaching me to appreciate the efficacy of the subtle threat.

Terri Elders

The Connection

It is good to have an end to journey toward, but it is the journey that matters in the end.

Ursula K. LeGuin

"Mom," I hollered as I headed out the kitchen door, "I'm going to play in the hayloft with the baby kittens." Warm, soft dust squished between my bare toes as I bounded across the barnyard, into the barn, and scrambled up the hayloft ladder. I was surprised to see my big brother slumped on a hay bale, his denim-clad elbows resting on his knees, holding his head in his hands.

"What's the matter, Junior?" I asked anxiously. He didn't move or answer. His despair was so deep and acute it scared me. I wanted to say or do something to help him. But I was just a little sister, and Junior was ten years older, more like an uncle than a brother. Slowly I walked over and sat on the hay bale beside him.

Grabbing hold of his overalls' strap I pleaded, "Tell me what's wrong." Junior ran his fingers through his thick black hair and shook his head. His despair swirled around us and settled in my heart. At that moment, the age difference between my brother and me melted like candle wax. I felt a great connection with him and wanted to comfort him, but I didn't have the words. Forgetting all about the kittens, I sat quietly beside him. Silence filled the loft. Time passed. Soon, the late afternoon sun filtered between the silvered boards of the battered barn wall. Junior never said a word, not even to ask me to leave.

When I heard our mother calling me, I stood and touched his shoulder. I offered timidly, "It will be alright, Junior." Then I climbed swiftly down the loft ladder and ran to the house. That night in bed I pondered the day's events. It would be years before I understood the reason for Junior's unhappiness.

That afternoon in the loft was the turning point in an ongoing battle between Junior and our father. Junior wanted to enlist in the army and join his three brothers overseas. Dad didn't want him to go: Junior was exempt because he was needed on the family farm. Every day Junior put his enlistment papers in the mailbox, and every day Dad took them out. Finally, Dad relented. The enlistment papers stayed in the mailbox and Junior's orders came. Junior was ecstatic.

He began six intensive weeks of training, and then he was on his way to Germany to fight in the Battle of the Bulge. His first letters were full of the excitement of training and travel. Then the letters stopped coming.

One snowy winter evening a telegram from the War Department was delivered to our house. The taxicab driver wept when he handed the long, brown envelope to my father. My mother began to weep and wail. After many months, my father replaced the blue star displayed in our window with a gold star. Neighbors stopped by to give their condolences.

Time has dimmed the loss, the sorrow, and the weeping. But time cannot erase that chance afternoon when a connection was forged between a big brother and a little sister.

Norma Favor

When Cows Fly

Imagination is the true magic carpet.

Norman Vincent Peale

In the late 1950s when my sister, Janice, and I were kids, we fantasized that we lived on a huge horse ranch complete with stables, corrals, and miles of white-painted fences. Our pretend-ranch was easy to imagine because we already lived on a small farm; however, the five-acre parcel consisted only of our house, a hay barn, and a cow pasture. For animals we had a mongrel dog named Be-bop, two Hereford cows—Lucy and Ethel—and a Guernsey steer known as Frisky.

Janice and I were not satisfied with just having cattle on our ranch, so we kept pestering our father to get us a horse. He said he would think about it, and then added jokingly that if we wanted a horse bad enough we should practice riding the cows. We thought Dad was serious, so we tried our luck with Lucy and Ethel, but neither cow would stand still long enough for us to climb aboard. Frisky was much more accommodating because he didn't run away from anybody. He was so docile and listless that we thought about changing his name to Zombie.

When I lifted Janice onto Frisky's back, he took two steps forward, then put his head down and began grazing. This was no way for a cowboy to ride the range, and Frisky obviously didn't understand his role in our sister/brother fantasy. To get Frisky moving, Janice jammed her heels into his ribs. Frisky weakly responded by swinging his tail across Janice's back, as if swatting a bothersome fly. Then I plucked a handful of green grass and waved it under Frisky's nose, but he ignored me as well. Our only alternative was to bring in the dog.

We normally kept Be-bop chained to the bumper of a junked car, letting him loose on the weekends for exercise and romance. Since we were the last house on a dead-end road, Be-bop didn't have many opportunities to chase cars, so whenever he was free, he went into the pasture and chased the cattle. With Janice sitting high on top of Frisky, I turned Be-bop loose.

When Be-bop ran into the pasture, he was puzzled at the sight of Janice perched on Frisky's back. Then Be-bop went berserk, howling and nipping at Frisky's legs. Frisky took off like a rocket and after two leaping bounds, a screaming Janice bounced to the ground, narrowly missing a fresh cow pie. Be-bop continued the chase, also stampeding Lucy and Ethel. We figured that Be-bop thought Frisky had captured Janice and it was his job to set her free. Since he offered no speed control, we never used the dog again.

Then we remembered that when our mother worked in the garden, she sometimes threw unwanted vegetables into the pasture and the cattle would go crazy over them. Cabbage seemed to be their favorite, so we plucked a ripe head to entice Frisky. It worked perfectly. One of us led Frisky with the cabbage head while the other rode. When we finished riding for the day, we hid the cabbage in the barn.

Early the next morning, Frisky's loud bellowing awakened us. He was on the second floor of the barn standing at the edge of the loft door. Janice and I had left the pasture gate open, which allowed Frisky to go inside the barn to look for the cabbage. During his search, Frisky climbed up the stairs but could not get back down. So now we had to figure out a way to get the 800-pound steer off the second floor!

We couldn't send Frisky down the stairs because he was likely to get seriously injured. We had but one option: Frisky would have to jump. Dad parked his truck under the door then loaded it with hay bales. Frisky looked down at the hay padding and bellowed, as if he was aware of the acrobatics we had in mind. Dad and I pushed Frisky's rump while Janice sat on the truck roof waving the cabbage head. We'll never know if it was the cabbage or Dad twisting Frisky's tail that made him jump, but he leaped out the second-story door and miraculously landed in the truck, unhurt.

Dad left Frisky on the truck and drove him away, telling us that Frisky was going to another farm where he would be happier. What we didn't know was that Dad took him to the slaughterhouse.

About two weeks later, we were having steak for supper. Janice and I began complaining that we missed Frisky and asked if we'd ever see him again. Dad almost choked on our question, but Mom was quick to calm us when she said, "Don't worry, kids, someday Frisky will turn up when you least expect him."

Arthur Wiknik, Jr.

Berrily Made It

I once read an interesting feature in *Time* magazine. The writer claimed that though your parents may raise you, it's your brothers and sisters who shape you.

Growing up in the 1960s in a family with ten siblings, I can certainly vouch for the fact that my brothers and sisters were my protectors, goads, tormentors, playmates, counselors, sources of envy, and objects of pride. My siblings served as an instruction manual on how to have relationships with others, and they continue to fine-tune me on how I interact with others to this day.

My brother Gene and I probably gave Mom and Dad the most grief as we spoke our minds and demanded independence. We were close in age and temperament. We both even considered entering the religious life as our careers, but then we realized being a nun or priest wouldn't work for us—we didn't take orders well.

To understand the relationship between Gene and me, you must venture back with me into childhood. Back then, it didn't take a genius to figure out that he saw me as a direct rival to Mom and Dad's attention. When I was a baby, he turned over my bassinet trying to steal my rattle. Over the years, try as I might, he never included me in his fun, especially when I was eight years old and he was nine.

It was during that time that Gene and my brothers built a tree house and wouldn't let me help. Afterward, he tacked up a sign that read, "Girls Not Allowed." I tattled to Mom about his tree house. Usually Mom didn't pay much attention to tattling, so I was surprised when she yelled at him to come home.

"Gene, Diana tells me that you built a tree house at the end of the field."

"That's right," Gene said, just as proud as you please. "It's in the trees way over there." He pointed into the distance.

"Now Gene," Mom began sternly, "that tree is too close to the railroad tracks. You could fall off a limb right onto the barbed-wire fence. The county put that fence there to keep kids away from the tracks."

"Ah, Mom, I made a platform in it and everything. The guys love it. If you let us keep it, I promise that I'll make everyone clear out of it when a train goes by."

Mom was quiet for a minute. Surely she wouldn't fall for that line of gobbledy-gook. I couldn't believe it when she said, "Okay, but keep on this side of the fence. No one goes near the tracks and, oh, let Diana play in the tree house."

As it turned out, the tree house was nice enough, but Gene, my other brothers, and his friends made my life so miserable that I didn't stay long. Besides, I had other things to do. That morning, Mom had promised that if I picked a bucket of wild raspberries, I could make fresh raspberry sauce. There is nothing in the world like fresh, sweetened raspberries to scoop over a bowl of yummy vanilla ice cream.

So I ran back to the house and grabbed the bucket. The wild raspberry bushes near the house were nice enough and the bees not too disturbing, so I picked there for a while. But these berries were small compared with the acre of raspberries in that forbidden territory around the railroad tracks.

Making sure that no one was watching, I dashed back to the barbed-wire fence until I found where the wire sagged. Carefully, I stepped over the prickly fence and onto the gravel next to the tracks. There were green bushes with bright red raspberries, some as big as a penny, just ripe for the picking. I battled the bees and began to fill my bucket.

When I heard the faint sound of a train whistle in the distance, my heart began to race. *It's okay,* I told myself, *just find the low spot in the fence and climb over.* But I couldn't find the low spot. I raced back and forth along the fence. It seemed as though the sag had disappeared. The ground began to shake. The air was filled with the loud whine of the train's engine. Panicking, I stuck my head through the barbed wire and pulled my arms through. My shirt and pants were caught on the prickly thorns. I think I was screaming, but the train drowned me out.

Then I felt someone's hand grab mine and give it a mighty tug. I didn't budge. The train was now inches away. The hand that was pulling me let go and two arms quickly appeared, reaching around my torso and hugging me. I buried my head into a bony shoulder, closed my eyes, and cried. The train whizzed by so close that I swear it brushed my backside.

Then all was quiet. I lifted up my head and brushed away my tears. I was so embarrassed. But my brother Gene looked even more embarrassed.

"Now look what you did! I'm bleeding!" he whined.

"I didn't make you hold me," I replied, worried how I would explain my own scratches.

"Fraidy cat, crybaby," Gene said.

"Squirrel bait!" I retaliated.

Carrying the bucket, I pulled myself carefully through the rest of the fence and raced home. We never talked about what happened. Surprisingly, Mom never asked about our wounds. But I think she figured out the act of brotherly chivalry when I gave Gene, my arch nemesis, an extra scoop of berries on his ice cream that night.

Diana M. Amadeo

"I love family reunions, except for when mom punishes us for arguing, sis."

He's Mine

Things turn out best for people who make the best of the way things turn out.

John Wooden

"Nana, do you like Will?" our three-year-old granddaughter asked as we drove her home from the hospital the night her brother was born.

"Oh, yes, I do, Mary. He looks like you when you were born."

"I'm going to keep him," she replied from her toddler chair in the back seat of the car. "He's mine."

"Are you going to share him with Mommy and Daddy and the rest of us?" I questioned her.

Silence. And then, "Okay, but he's mine."

"I know, honey."

And I did. I understood more than she realized. My brother was "mine" too. I asked for him, and even threatened to run away from home if Mother didn't produce a baby brother by my fifth birthday. The fact that it was wartime and Daddy was in the hospital recovering from serious wounds made no difference in my young mind. I wanted a baby brother and nothing else would do.

Somehow, my parents managed to come through, only a month after my deadline. It was a difficult breech birth, one that almost killed Mother and caused the nurses to think the baby was born dead, until he began to cry on his own after being put aside so they could work on her. He was tough and began his life by showing it.

On the day they brought him home from the hospital, I was allowed to stay home from kindergarten. I took every doll, stuffed animal, and toy I owned and lined them around the living room wall of our small apartment. I was excited about playing with my brother.

But he didn't play. He just lay there, sleeping in his bassinet. He didn't talk or walk. He didn't do anything but eat, sleep, and cry. This wasn't what I'd ordered at all. I was dreadfully disappointed. But he was cute. And he was "mine."

In time, baby Steve began to respond to me with gummy smiles. I found it easy to make him happy by sticking my dirty finger in his mouth. It's a wonder he didn't come down with some dreadful disease, but he thrived. A few months later, he was getting into my things. I wailed to my mother about it. "You wanted him, don't complain to me," was always the response. "You work it out."

Years flew by, and I became my brother's advocate, standing up for him against bullies on the playground, even teachers who dared to discipline him. Didn't they know he was mine?

As we grew, our age difference took us in diverse directions. I cheered him on as he raced his go-carts; he gave thumbs up or down to my dates. And we endured our loss of Daddy without words but by just holding onto each other and sharing Mother's grief. The following year I helped him get dressed for my wedding so he could give me away.

Then we were apart. For years, as I traveled with my Navy husband to ports around the world, we only communicated by letter or phone. When we returned, Steve was in the service in Vietnam and our years apart expanded, especially since we settled in the West and he returned to the Southeast.

Whenever we were able to get together for family gatherings, however, we bickered and laughed, and I called him my "baby brother" to the amusement of my children and his.

My daughter interrupted my reverie.

"Mary, go stop your brother from crying," she said to her now four-year-old daughter.

We knew the instant she walked into his line of sight because we heard six-month-old baby laughter. She was his "favorite thing."

Yes, he was "hers," no doubt about it, just as my brother is still "mine."

Jean Stewart

Look After Sissy

At age five, I was learning the meaning of "caution." I had received a mechanical skunk as a gift. I could put a key into a hole in his side, wind him up, and he'd walk forward, stop, and look side to side while shaking his long plume of a tail. A sign around his neck read "Caution."

Sam, my older and wiser brother, already knew its meaning. He was eight and I thought that made him smarter. Since he was older and supposedly wiser, Sam was often admonished by Mother to "look after Sissy."

Sam and I grew up in the 1950s on a small farm in southwestern Virginia and often smelled the telling stink of a disturbed skunk. Mountain people called skunks polecats. By either name, a sniff of its potent musk could last a lifetime.

Sometimes we'd see a polecat in the field. Ours were black with dual white stripes down their backs, ending in bushy tails like Persian cats. Beady black eyes stared from their weasel-shaped faces. I thought they were pretty, but we'd been warned to keep our distance.

One day Daddy came into the kitchen where Mother was churning butter, and we overheard him tell her there was a polecat in the cellar. He couldn't figure out how it got down there, but Daddy had left the door propped open, hoping it would leave on its own.

Sam and I looked at each other—this we had to see! Covered steps led down to the cellar beneath the smoke-house, where jars of canned goods and crates of potatoes, rutabagas, and turnips were stored. Sometimes on hot days, Sam and I would sneak into the cellar to get cool. We delighted in the dank smell of the dirt, but were afraid of the darkness.

I loved cats, real ones, and that day I was carrying a gentle gray tabby. She purred contently in my arms. Toting her, I followed my brother down the cellar steps. He carefully poked his head around the door. Seeing no polecat, Sam went in, with me on his heels. A trace of light glimmered through the cobwebs covering the window high on the wall. As our eyes became accustomed to the darkness, we saw Mother's canning jars on the dirt shelf to the left. A few crates of sprouting potatoes were on the floor to the right.

"I don't see him," I complained.

"Over there," said Sam as he pointed to a dark shape in the corner, its camouflage betrayed by its white stripes. The polecat stared at us, and us at it, and none of us moved.

The stare down continued until I—who to this day can't imagine why—tossed the tabby, her startled paws claw-ing the air seeking traction, directly onto the polecat. Tangled fur tumbled and scratched until the tabby finally freed herself and took flight. I giggled—briefly. Then that polecat turned its tail to us and drenched me, my barefoot brother, and the turbine tabby with its whole load of potent musk. Phew! Struggling to breathe, we raced to the kitchen.

Mother stopped churning butter. Scrunching her face, she gasped, "Where have you been? Get out of here!"

She made us strip outside and filled the metal tub on

the porch for a bath, even though it wasn't Saturday. Daddy buried our clothes.

After the bath, my brother looked at me and said, "You stink."

I sniffed and asserted, "No, you're the one who stinks!"

Daddy didn't take us to church that Sunday, or the next. For some time both our parents would have flunked the question: "Have you hugged your child today?"

The tabby remained in self-imposed exile for an extended period. Eventually she returned, but ran if I tried to pick her up. The polecat vanished, but I wouldn't be surprised if the cellar still stinks.

I rarely played with my mechanical skunk after that, but when I did, I made sure his tail was pointed away from me. I learned what the word "caution" meant, and I suspect Sam's definition of caution includes something about the challenge of watching out for an unpredictable younger sister.

Lucile C. Cason

Raincoats and Regrets

When you make the finding yourself—even if you're the last person on Earth to see the light—you'll never forget it.

Carl Sagan

"Happy birthday, Tim!" Aunt Marge stood just inside the front door as she handed a gaily-wrapped package to my brother. Tim's eyes sparkled as he grabbed the present and immediately started a chorus of, "Can I open it now, please? Can I? Can I?"

From the size of the box, I guessed that it was clothing and instantly felt sorry for my little brother. There wasn't an eight-year-old around who could get excited about that. But my brother, full of innocent exuberance, never once suspected the package's contents as he ripped through the wrappings and discovered—clothing. And not just any clothing, but a shiny, banana-yellow raincoat with a matching hat! Tim held it up for all to see and feigned a weak smile as Aunt Marge beamed with delight.

She's clueless, I thought. But we had manners, so I didn't laugh out loud and my brother gave her a dutiful hug.

After Aunt Marge left, I slipped into my brother's room carrying the raincoat.

"It's not all bad, Tim. Look, it has a secret pocket! See?" I envisioned all the swell things it could hold, like Charleston Chews. My mouth watered just thinking about our favorite candy. The only problem was money, or rather, the lack of it.

Dad was a salesman and lately there weren't enough commissions, which meant no allowance. Tim and I missed our trips to our favorite five and dime, Ben Franklin—a treasure trove of assorted goodies. For kids with an allowance to spend, that is.

I thought about our friend, Denise, who always had plenty of candy. Her allowance had to be huge, until she told me she'd stolen it all, convincing me it was easy. And that's how it all started—my big idea, I mean.

I smirked. "Tim, I've got a plan for this ridiculous raincoat." His eyes grew wide as I filled him in on the details.

"Nuh-uh, Sister Bernadette said that's a sin," he said with a look of superiority and a finger waving furiously.

My little brother needed to learn the finer details about sin, and as his older sister it was up to me to teach him. After all, I was eleven and had the Catholic scale all figured out. I explained to my brother that sins were rated from "somewhat bad" to "really awful." You needn't worry unless you committed a mortal sin. Then look out, you'd burn in hell. But a venial sin? That could be remedied in the confessional; you say you're sorry, do two Our Father's and one Hail Mary. No sweat.

The next day, with Tim buckled into the yellow raincoat, we headed for Ben Franklin's, all set for "Operation Charleston Chew."

I gave him a final briefing at the door, "Just look normal. I'll put the candy into your secret pocket, you leave, and I'll follow in a couple of minutes."

In the candy aisle, nerves humming, I grabbed a bag of Charleston Chews, took a quick glance around, and slipped it into his pocket. "Go!" My heart thundered as Tim took off. I ducked down another aisle and peeked around before heading for the exit. That was easy! I could taste that candy already, until . . .

"Stop right there!" Mr. Richardson, the store manager, towered above me, red-faced, with Tim at his side. *Busted! This isn't supposed to happen. Denise said it was a cinch!* Mr. Richardson led us to his office and picked up the phone to call our mother. No amount of begging could get him to change his mind.

We were in big trouble, all for a stupid bag of candy. Mom picked us up and apologized to Mr. Richardson. Back at the house, she sent us upstairs with a fatal warning, "Just wait until your father gets home." We trudged up the steps, sentenced to solitary confinement. My mind was in a quandary. I was supposed to know better. Hadn't my parents always taught me right from wrong? *Darn that Denise.*

Finally, the dreaded moment arrived.

"Susan, Timothy. Come down here."

Uh-oh, Dad was home.

I slung a protective arm around my brother's shoulders as we slowly entered the dining room. Dad cleared his throat, an unspoken command to look at him when he spoke. But it was hard to keep our eyes on him because the sun was glaring through the window behind him.

That's when it hit me. *No wonder we got caught! It was a beautiful day and it had been all day. What idiots! Who wears a raincoat on a sunny day? We may as well have announced it: WE'RE HERE TO STEAL!*

Dad's voice cut through my revelation. "I didn't know I'd raised two thieves for children." Contempt rang in every word. We stood there, heads hung in disgrace, awaiting our sentencing. But all we got was a soft whisper, "I'm so disappointed in you. Go on, now, wash your hands for supper."

My face burned with shame and my stomach somersaulted as we slunk into the bathroom and turned on the faucet. I wondered if my little brother felt as wretched as I did.

We dried our hands and shuffled back into the dining room. There was silence as Mom passed around mashed potatoes and Dad cut the roast. Tim slouched over his plate, and I worried that he'd never forgive me.

After supper I went to his room and plopped down on the bed next to him. "I'm sorry I got you in trouble. Guess that was a pretty stupid idea."

"Well, I went along with it." he said, looking glum. "Guess we're both dopes."

We sat and talked and agreed that from now on Denise could have her ill-gotten booty. Stealing was for losers. And so were yellow raincoats. Together, we wadded that yellow raincoat up into a little ball and shoved it into the deepest corner of Tim's closet, happy that our life of crime was over.

Susan Karas

"Mr. Erskine, your bratty little sister is
on the line with a takeover offer."

The Yo-Yo and the Snowball

Walking up to the grocery store that summer afternoon, I was proud to have saved enough money for Steve's birthday present. He was worth it. Sure, he was the kind of brother who would chase me away when he and his friends were playing football, but that was okay because I really didn't want to play anyhow. He was also the kind of brother who would take a big chunk out of his paper-route money just to buy me—or give me the exact amount of cash for—the very thing I'd always wanted, and he always knew what it was.

It was the 1950s, so my fifty-cent allowance gave me plenty of money for a great gift. I held my allowance tightly in my sweaty hand, knowing that I had to get him something special. I went up and down each aisle. First there was the vegetable aisle, but I knew he wouldn't want a head of lettuce or even a shiny red apple. Then I walked down the macaroni aisle. I knew there was nothing there for him either.

Every aisle was beginning to look the same until I reached the cookie aisle. There were all kinds of snack cakes, like Twinkies, Ring Dings, and Devil Dogs, but I didn't remember him really liking any of those. Then I came to the Snowballs. I was sure Steve would think they were neat. I know I always did. I fingered the Snowball package, noticing the blue-stamped price of twelve cents on the back. I smiled to myself. Holding the cellophane package in my free hand, I admired the two big pink treats made of deep, dark, delicious devil's food cake stuffed with a rich creamy center, wrapped in a marshmallow and coconut topping. I said out loud, "He'll love them."

Now that I already would be spending a lot of my money on the cakes, I was beginning to worry about buying him his other present. So I continued down the aisles of the very small store, but everything cost a lot more than I had.

After getting in line and paying my twelve cents for the Snowballs, all I had left of my allowance was thirty-eight cents. I realized that maybe snack cakes were not really a special present, so I started to worry. *Maybe I should go next door to the candy store,* I told myself.

As soon as I opened the door, I saw a counter covered with yo-yos. They were red, blue, green, and black shiny flat balls with a ring of string hanging from each one. On another table there were some neat dark brown ones made of wood, with the words "Dunkin Yo-yo" stamped on their fronts. I knew that name from the television commercials, and I hoped that my brother did, too.

While I was standing at the counter, a man from the store came over and asked if he could help me. I told him I was looking for a present for my brother whose thirteenth birthday was today. The man thought that a yo-yo would be the perfect gift and he began demonstrating it. He moved the string, with the heavy flat ball that was attached to it, up and down. I was so envious and wished that I knew how to do it, too. But I really believed he was an expert because he was a man—and yo-yos were really boy things. That's the way they were portrayed on the television commercials.

"Mister, how much is the dark brown wooden one you were using?" I asked.

"Oh, this is your lucky day. They're on special for only fifty cents."

"Well, you see I only have thirty-eight cents because I already bought my brother a package of Snowballs. You know, the marshmallow- and coconut-covered cakes with the dark chocolate cake and creamy center? See?" I said, holding the pink package up close to his face.

"That's alright, young lady. You can have it for thirty-eight cents."

Excited, I dug down deep into my dungaree pocket, handed the man the rest of my money, and skipped out the door. I left with my two bags and a big smile that lasted all the way to my front door. Now the problem was to sneak into the house without my smile, which I really had a hard time getting rid of.

I almost succeeded, up until the moment I met my brother sitting on our step. "What's so funny?" he said.

"Oh, nothing," I lied. Then I handed him a bag.

"What's this?"

"Happy birthday!"

Steve opened the first bag and said it was just what he wanted, ripping into the sweet cake. Then I handed him the other.

"Cool! How'd you know I wanted one of these?"

"Well, I kinda knew what they were from the TV commercial I saw the other day," I said, still grinning.

"You mean you saw it too? And you paid attention? I'm surprised because I thought yo-yos were just for guys. At least that's what they showed on TV."

"Yeah, I know, but even if I am a girl, I would like to try it sometime, if it's okay with you? Maybe I could go back to the store where I bought it and ask the man to show me how."

"Don't be silly, sis. I'll teach you. Just watch," my brother said, placing the string carefully around my finger and helping me make the flat wooden ball go down and up, and down and up.

"You know, Steve, you're the best brother in the world."

"That's really not the truth, but I am having the best birthday."

Fay Ulanoff

8

INSIGHTS AND LESSONS

My advice to you is not to inquire why or whither, but just enjoy your ice cream while it's on your plate.

Thornton Wilder

Keep On Truckin'

Do what you can, with what you have, where you are.

Theodore Roosevelt

When I was in my twenties, a friend asked me, "What type of person are you?" I had one of those fly-catching, gaping-mouth moments as I stumbled for an answer. All I wanted back then was to be "cool."

I've learned many lessons growing up, but the biggest lesson in my life came from an unlikely source—my oldest sister. Born with spina bifida, Janet wasn't supposed to live past her first day of life, but she came out fighting and has been doing so for fifty-seven-plus years.

Two decades later, I have an honest answer to that long-ago posed question: I am a 1957 Chevrolet pickup. For those not familiar with old cars, a '57 Chevy is a really nice truck, a true workingman's truck. And Janet is this classic truck, too.

Originally, I wanted to be a Ferrari. They're the "cool people" of the car world—those nice, spiffy, drop-your-jaw, gorgeous cars that get polished each time they're taken out of the garage. Pampered each day of their existence, they never want for anything.

But by watching my sister, I have learned that I'm a pickup, not a sports car.

From the very first day of her life, Janet proved the doctors wrong by surviving. After that, the doctors explained the things she would never be able to do, like walk, communicate, thrive, bond, cook, keep a checkbook, or live on her own. The list was endless, but throughout her life, she did them all. She was always out in front, keeping her head down, constantly moving forward, regardless of whether she had to go uphill or downhill in life.

One memorable "moving forward" event occurred when I was in junior high and Janet was in high school.

"I want to ski," she announced one day.

I looked at her, smiled, and said, "Okay, I'll teach you."

It took lots of work, but finally she was able to ski, turning and stopping on her own. By the end of the first year, Janet was able to ski her favorite runs without help. Once again, she checked off another box on her list of things she wasn't supposed to be able to do. I was so proud of her.

After graduating from high school, with minimal help and allowances (another accomplishment to check off her list), Janet entered the work force, walking to work each day because she was unable to drive a car. She learned how to do her job as a cleaner at the local rest home and has done that same job with a smile for over thirty years.

As a pickup truck, my sister has a hard time understanding certain things, like being sick. When told to go home one day due to an illness, she became confused. "I can sit home and be sick or I can come to work and be sick. What's the difference?" she asked her supervisor.

That's my sister. If work needs to be done, she's going to do it. If something needs to be fixed, she's going to fix it. She's met every challenge in her life with the same

Chevy pickup truck tenacity, and rarely has she failed. While many go zipping along in their Ferraris, Janet is fighting for herself, digging deep into the well she has and coming up with pure, sweet water.

This is what I have learned from my sister: to keep trudging on, to dig deeper, and to truly pay attention to the wonders of my own life. Still, there are moments I wish I were a Ferrari. But that isn't the road Janet and I have the luxury to travel. It's up to us to get ourselves up the hills of life, like an old, reliable pickup truck.

As I write this, my sister is facing yet another daunting hill in her life. She was diagnosed with cancer—one of the worst kinds. She didn't crumble or fall to pieces. Not once through her surgery and chemotherapy did she complain. Janet told me, "Joe, God hasn't spoken yet. The only limitations I have are the ones I put on myself or the ones I let others talk me into."

I'm proud of my big sister. Overcoming the obstacles of her disability through sheer perseverance and joy, Janet has shown me how to be the very best 1957 Chevrolet pickup I can be. Thanks, sis.

Joe Lair

Reprinted by permission of Jay Max. ©2007 Jay Max.

The Haircut Makes the Boy

Assumptions allow the best in life to pass you by.

John Sales

When I was a child, I just knew that Daddy loved my brother more than me. I could tell. Daddy let my little brother go with him to the hardware store and to roofing jobs, and I always seemed to be left behind. Daddy showed my little brother how to build things and even let him use the hammer and saw. I simply stood in the shadows and watched the two of them participate in father-and-son activities. How I longed for Daddy to take me fishing and toss the ball to me in the backyard! But I knew deep in my heart that it would never happen because I was nothing but a girl.

That's when I got a great idea: I would turn myself into a boy! After all, my brother and I looked so much alike. The only real difference was that he had short, sandy blond hair, while mine was long. *If I got my hair cut like my brother, Daddy would have two sons,* I thought. I could even get my hair cut at the same barbershop that Daddy and my brother used. It would be perfect!

I could barely wait for haircut day to come. Finally, Daddy announced one morning that he and my brother were going in for their trims.

"Please, can I come, too?" I begged.

"Are you sure you want to come to the barber shop? Don't you want to stay here and play with your sister?" he asked.

"Oh no, sir," I answered without a moment's hesitation. "I want to go with you."

I was delighted when Daddy said that I could go. I slid in the front seat of the truck between the two of them and felt like a part of the team. Of course, I had not yet mentioned my plan to him. As we drove down the highway, I twirled a long blond pigtail between my fingers, imagining what my new life of hammers and nails and puppy-dog tails would be like.

In just a few short minutes, Daddy pulled into a parking spot right in front of the barbershop. I marched in with my father and brother, the only female in sight, and stood behind Daddy as he greeted the other customers. Suddenly, I felt just a little bit out of place in this man's world of shaving cream, razors, and aftershave. I swallowed hard and watched as my little brother climbed expertly into the barber's chair. While Daddy carried on conversations with the other gentlemen, I gathered the courage to ask him if I could get a haircut too. Finally, during a lull in the discussions, I tapped my father on the shoulder.

"Daddy," I said, my voice quivering ever so slightly.

"What is it, sugar? You want to go get a piece of bubble gum from the machine?" he asked, digging deep into his pockets.

"No sir. What I really want is a haircut like his," I said, pointing to my brother. I braced myself for my father's response.

Daddy looked at me with an expression of surprise. "That sounds like something you need to check with your momma about. Besides, you don't want to get your hair cut here, do you? Isn't that something you need to do at the beauty parlor?"

"Oh, but Daddy," I explained in a trembling voice, "I want a real haircut just like his!" I said, pointing once again to my brother.

Now it was Daddy's turn to swallow hard. "I don't know how your momma would feel about that. You sure do have some pretty hair and if you get it cut, there won't be any more ponytails and all." He looked at me with questioning eyes.

That's when the barber joined in. As my little brother scrambled down from the chair, the barber brushed the hair remnants off it and patted the seat. "Ah, come on and let her get a hair cut! It'll grow back out if she doesn't like it!"

Before Daddy had a chance to argue, I practically ran to the vinyl-covered chair and clamored into place. While Daddy had seemed perfectly relaxed when his son went under the scissors, he was tense when his little girl was beneath the clippers.

With a snip, snip here and a snip, snip, snip there, I watched my golden tresses slide to the floor. Suddenly, I was not so certain of my decision to become a boy. I gazed longingly at my long blond pigtails lying amid my brother's short trimmings. I imagined my mother's expression when I returned home with far less hair on my head than when I left. Every morning, she lovingly brushed my long hair and removed the knots and tangles. Then, with her expert fingers, she gently braided my silky locks or created a special up-do just for me. As I imagined my mother's reaction I regreted my decision. *What had I done? I wanted to be a girl again!* I closed my eyes to keep the tears from falling.

Before I could say another word, however, the barber whirled me around to face the wall-sized mirror. I gazed at the shorthaired stranger staring back at me. I truly did not know whether to laugh or cry. I turned to look at my brother and father, desperately needing their reassurance.

"Neat!" called my little brother. "You look like me!"

Daddy walked over and put his arms around me to lift me from the chair. "Sugar, you look cute as a button! Your momma is gonna love it."

Suddenly, the pit in my stomach did not feel nearly as deep.

"Hey, Daddy, can we have a penny for the bubble gum machine?" my brother asked, as Daddy took his turn in the same seat in which my brother and I had sat.

That "we" coming from my brother was music to my ears! The male bond I had so longed for finally existed, just as I had hoped! Any regrets were immediately dispelled. As we raced out the door, I heard a customer tell my father, "I declare, those two could pass for twins!"

Of course, one of our first team efforts was to get my new haircut past Momma. When the three of us—Daddy, my brother, and I—walked in the door, we did it together. And, though it took a little getting used to, Momma adjusted quickly and even seemed to like the ease of my new wash-and-wear look. She even agreed to let my sister get her long curls cut, too.

It was some time later that I discovered that the differences between boys and girls extended far beyond the length of their hair, and it didn't take too many male-bonding experiences for me to learn that hammers and nails were not really for me. I even realized that I didn't have to be a boy for Daddy to love me. Though we might not hammer and drill together, we shared experiences that are reserved exclusively for fathers and daughters. As for my brother, he recognized long before I did that I truly preferred the world of lace and bows and all things shiny to his more masculine world, and that was just fine with him. He was perfectly content for our play to consist of his G.I. Joe figures rescuing my Sunshine Family. Boy, do I hate it when my little brother is right!

Terri Duncan

A Little Pink Lie

One day during the summer of 1966, my mother bestowed upon me the very important responsibility of watching my little brother outside, while she watched *Dark Shadows*, her favorite scary soap.

My brother was just two and a half, still in diapers and nearly helpless. I was nine, nearly grown, and very capable. I stood outside on the curb of my all-concrete yard (we lived above a store) looking across the street at the neighbor kids' yard, a grassy green oasis with a brand new, red swing set. My brother was still inside, getting his shoes tied. Between him and me were two doors and two flights of steps.

I calculated—because I was nine and knew my multiplication tables by heart—that I had gobs of time to run over and play on the swing set before my toddling brother tromped down all those steps and I was stuck baby-sitting. After all, with his tiny legs, he had to do the old "one-two": carefully stretch one leg and dangling foot until it touched the step and found firm ground, then bring along his other leg and foot to join it. Then the whole thing was repeated again—one-two, one-two. Slow as molasses.

Calculations finished, I hopped off the curb, jetted across the street, climbed the fence, and lickety-split, I was pushing two kids on a glider and playing "let's touch the sky."

Who knows how many kid minutes went by before I looked over and saw my little brother heading toward me, about to do the "one-two" right off the curb and into the street, with a car heading in his direction! As I turned to start my mad dash to save him, the glider hit my face. I felt the sting, but there was no time for inspection. "Stop!" I screamed at him. "Don't move!"

I jumped the fence and skidded to a dead halt on the opposite curb from my brother. Our eyes met. The car whizzed past. I gulped. And in the beat of an eyelid, I saw him again—both feet in the street. His eyes were big, his mouth open, and he was frozen stiff from the wind of the big, metallic blur of the car.

I rushed to him, swung an arm around his waist, lifted him up, and set him down on the sidewalk. I bent down to scold him about cars and streets when he started pointing at my face, saying, "Boo boo. Boo boo."

I felt my cheek. It was wet. When I checked my hand, there was blood on my fingers. I looked down and there was blood on my white top with the yellow daisies. I was in big trouble. I wanted to run upstairs for medical treatment, but I didn't want to wind up getting the third degree. Even though I saved my brother, I disobeyed my mother. I was nine, not stupid.

I had to make up a story. One she'd believe. *I could say I fell down,* I thought. No. *I poked myself with a stick?* No. *A rock?* No. *My brother did it?* Hmmm. I thought a little more. *How? With his fingernails? That's it! He scratched me with his fingernails. Oh, but not on purpose. No. It was an accident. We were just playing.* Perfect.

Now that I had a solid story, I trudged upstairs with my

brother in tow. I joined his one-two cadence, which gave me time to work up a panicky cry.

"Oh, heavens!" Mom screamed when she saw me, leaving the scary television show people behind and bolting across the room. "What on earth happened to your face?"

I told my story as she rifled through the medicine cabinet looking for Band-Aids and iodine.

"Your brother?" she questioned. "With his fingernails?"

She dabbed my cheek a little too hard with a soapy cloth while scolding my brother. "Did you do this?

"Boo boo," he answered.

"I'll 'boo boo' you," she told him.

I reminded her it was just an accident. We were playing, like good brothers and sisters. Really we were. She bought it. I was in the clear. I had dodged a spanking, and so had my brother.

Days went by. A scab formed and fell off. I was left with a bright pink scar, a reminder of my lie, and a reminder of how I had saved my baby brother. I can still feel the sting, in my heart as well as on my face.

Later, I was back in the neighbor's yard, playing on the swing set. This time I was with my little brother, pushing him on the glider. My mother was there, too. She was talking with the other mother.

"How's Patsy's face?" the other mother asked. "Looks like it's healed up pretty good."

"Yes. She's fine," replied my mother.

"You know," the other mother continued, shaking her head. "That just scared me to death when Patsy got hit by the glider and Little Ray almost got hit by that car."

My eyes drifted over Mom's way. They met hers. The look on her face told me she'd put two and two together. But I continued to play innocent, as if I hadn't heard them. I pushed my brother on the glider.

"Fly high, touch the sky," I said in my big, nine-year-old sister voice. "But not too high. We must be careful."

And I hoped Mom would take pity on me when we got home. After all, I did save my brother, and I already had a scar.

Patsy Zettler

Two Regrets

The fragrance always stays in the hand that gives the rose.

Hada Bejar

I suppose that everyone sees their big brothers in different ways. Was yours the bully who teased and pestered you growing up? If so, I bet you know how to defend yourself because of his taunting. Was he the cool kid you always emulated? You thought that if you tried hard, maybe he and his friends would welcome you as one of their own. Or was he the one you cared for, protected, and nourished?

For me, my brother Thibault was all those things and more. He was older than me by two years, and he always picked on me. We fought like cats and dogs our entire childhood. Back then, I couldn't imagine a person being meaner to his little sister than my brother was to me. I remember times when our mom asked us to pose in pictures and Thibault would take me in his arms and give me a big hug for the photo. No feelings in the world outshone the ones when he revealed that he loved me.

As we grew into adolescence, Thibault seldom showed that he cared for me as a sister. Teenage years are framed by our peers, and in the search for independence, often times family gets pushed aside. For years, Thibault and I had very few meaningful interactions, yet I continued to reach for him, wait for the turn around, and hope for a great friendship. He left for college, giving me a kiss, a hug, and maybe an "I love you."

But I don't remember the "I love you." I remember running to my room after the farewell and crying for days because of the loss I felt in my heart. It was not until years later, when I visited Thibault for two weeks in South Africa, that we began to share more intimately the stories of our growing up, deeper emotions, and heretofore, untold thoughts. I realized during that trip that we were finally reaching the point where my older brother and I were becoming best friends. The feeling was like the hugs I looked forward to as a child and the camaraderie I had always wished for. What Thibault still never knew was that I sincerely loved him, that he represented so much for me and who I am, that he possessed the qualities I looked for in people, and that despite our years of ups and downs, he was still one of the most amazing people in my life.

One afternoon in Cape Town, he and I bought a bottle of wine, cheese, and crackers and drove down the coast to watch the sunset. We parked the car on the side of the road and walked down to the rim of a cliff that fell into the Indian Ocean. Before us, the sun painted the sky and water bright orange. It was at that moment when I decided to tell Thibault all the things I had never really said about his mentorship, friendship, and just how much I cared for him. He sat next to me, listened, and when I was finished speaking, we sat in silence for a long while.

At one point, without turning to look at me, Thibault said, "You know, Lauren, I have two regrets in life."

Without letting him finish, my mind began to wander and speculate as to all the things my brother could possibly have done and that his only two regrets must have been colossal from what I knew of him growing up.

He spoke about having made many mistakes in his life and how he looked at them all as growing experiences— but that there were two he would take back if he could. The first was not having been the boyfriend his first love deserved, a regret that I expected. The other regret took him a long while to declare.

"Lauren," he finally began, "I was a jerk growing up. I did not respect the family as much as I should have, and I walked around like I owned the world. I remember once when I was with a friend and we had gotten intoxicated. After sobering up, we realized how foolish we had been. He and I decided that in order to make up for our senselessness, we were going to visit everyone we loved, give them hugs, and let them know how much we cared for them."

He continued describing how they drove around into the night seeing friends, finally returning home at 1:00 AM. Thibault decided that I would be his last and most important hug and kiss, because he wanted to finally tell me that he truly loved me. He said that he stood outside of my bedroom door in the wee hours of the morning for one hour, with his fist held up, ready to knock, until, flooded with emotion and full of shame, he fell to his knees and cried.

"I was too much of a coward to tell you how much I loved you," he said, "and how proud of you I was, how I thought you were beautiful and the best sister in the world. I couldn't do it because I was so wrapped up in myself. For years, Lauren, I wanted to reach out to you, and it is only now, as we sit together in the setting sun of paradise, that I can tell you my biggest regret in the world is not having been a more devoted brother to you."

Those hugs he gave me as a child had made me feel like a million dollars. The boy I looked up to as being the greatest guy on earth had accepted me. For years, unconsciously, I had waited for the moment when Thibault would tell me that he loved me as much as I loved him. That evening, under the most brilliant sky I had ever seen, with water reflecting every shade of yellow, pink, purple, and orange, my heart, which had yearned to be accepted by my big brother, was bursting at the seams. After what seemed to be a lifetime of watching Thibault's life run parallel with mine, yet with little acknowledgement from him, we finally began, at that moment, to walk on the same path as the friends I had always dreamed of us becoming.

Lauren Manekin

The Dragon Kite

There are no mistakes, no coincidences. All events are blessings given to us to learn from.
Elizabeth Kübler-Ross

"Looks like there's gonna be good wind blowing today." Terry picked up a handful of grass, tossed it into the air, and watched a gust of wind carry it away, tossing and twirling it. "Sure wish I had a kite."

"You got any of your allowance left?" I asked my older brother.

"Nah. I had to get an inner tube for my bike. Took every penny I had except seven cents."

"I got my allowance left."

"So?"

"So, I don't want to go kite flying by myself, silly."

"You mean you'd buy me a kite, too?"

"Sure. Why wouldn't I?"

"Gosh, Sis, you're the best."

"Just remember that next time you get mad at me." I chided him. "And you have to be the one who goes in to ask Momma if we can go up to the dime store."

Within minutes, Terry and I were on our way uptown on a mission to find the two best kites that fifty cents could buy.

It didn't take Terry long to make his choice. Right in front of the barrel was a bright red, blue, and yellow kite, with a big "S" right in the middle.

"Superman. That'll be easy to see when it's really up there."

I, however, was slower to choose. There weren't any kites with themes for girls. Just as I was ready to give up and take the plain yellow kite, I caught sight of a rainbow-colored kite with a black and white dragon right in the middle.

"Wow. Would you look at that?" I pulled the kite from the barrel.

"Boy, I'd say that's bright alright. Good choice." Terry's approval sealed the deal.

It wasn't long before Terry and I were in the field behind the military academy with our kites flying high in the air. Now and then, a cadet or an officer would stop for a moment and watch as the kites zigged and zagged back and forth across the sky as the wind tossed them about.

I decided to see just how high I could get my kite to sail, so I let out the full length of one roll of string and part of another.

"I think you ought to reel it in some," Terry cautioned after a few minutes. "The wind's picking up. Your string could break and you could lose your kite."

"Okay," I agreed and started winding my string around the stick. "My arms are getting tired anyway, and I'm hungry."

"Yeah, me too. We can always come back tomorrow."

Terry brought his kite in, laid it on the ground, and weighed it down with his canteen to keep it from blowing across the field.

My kite, however, was still over a hundred feet in the air when a strong gust blew in, yanking hard, pulling the string taut. Suddenly the string snapped. As the string drifted slowly to the ground, the paper dragon soared higher and higher, farther and farther away until it disappeared from sight.

"Gee, Sis, I'm sorry." Terry took my stick and finished reeling in the string. When he reached the end of the string, he held it up for my inspection. "Your string didn't break. It came untied."

"Guess next time I won't be in such a hurry and I'll tie a better knot."

"Come on, Mom's probably got something to eat waiting for us by now."

Terry was right. Momma had made a pot of her famous creamy potato and leek soup.

"Did you two have fun flying your kites today?"

"Yessum, we did, that is until I lost my kite."

"Did the string break?"

"No ma'am. I just didn't tie the knot good enough."

"What a shame. Well, these things happen." Momma reached over and rumpled my hair. "And did you learn anything from that?"

"Not to be in such a hurry, so I do things right and I'm not sorry later?"

"By Jove, I think you've got it. And I'm really sorry you lost your kite, Sissy."

Momma's little life lessons always stuck because of the gentle and kind way she had of pointing things out to Terry and me, never being judgmental or cross.

"Just think of it this way," Terry said. "Somebody somewhere is going to look out their door and find a paper dragon hanging around in their yard, waiting to be rescued." What a fun thought!

Sunday morning dawned like an angry lion. The sky

was filled with billowing white and gray thunderheads, and there was an ominous rumbling overhead. Now and then, a burst of light exploded behind the clouds that threatened to burst open in a downpour at any moment.

Momma stuffed our raincoats, umbrellas, and rain boots into her large tote and off to church we went. As we neared the grand brick structure, we noticed a group of people standing outside, some of them pointing toward the steeple.

"Well, will you look at that!" Terry exclaimed.

"I'll be darned," I added.

Halfway down the spire on the steeple was the dragon kite, the dragon pierced through and through.

"I wonder if that was what the preacher had in mind when he said we needed to learn to slay the dragons in our life," Momma chuckled, and gently nudged us toward the church doors.

Sheila Vincent-Bright

I'm Not Kate

Since the first day of my freshman year of high school, I heard the same thing over and over: "Oh, you're Kate's brother!" The teachers would read my name, then smile broadly and nod, like they were thinking of some movie star or rock icon. But they were really thinking about my sister and her academic success.

I knew the teachers would expect great things from me, too. I did well in school, but I felt I could never measure up to Kate. I didn't want to spend every minute reading or researching reports. Not like Kate. When assigned an eight-page essay, she'd write ten. And hand it in early. She took statistics classes at the local university *just for fun!* She even graduated valedictorian. Now she was studying at an Ivy League university.

Nothing I did seemed as good as Kate. Yeah, I got my share of As. But sometimes a few Bs stood out, like bruises on a perfect yellow banana. Now, Bs aren't so bad, unless you have a straight-A sister like Kate.

"Time to hand in your chemistry labs," said my teacher one morning. I took my work out of my notebook and smiled; chemistry was one of my best subjects. But the next week when I got back my paper, there was a big, red

eighty-nine at the top—a respectable grade, but not out-
standing. My work was good, but not as good as Kate's.

At the end of the year, awards were presented in each
subject. I sat in the auditorium anxiously awaiting the
math award. I'd scored in the 90s on every test, and 100 on
my final exam. One of my friends turned and nudged me
in the side. "You're a sure bet for this!" he said. My teacher
stood up to announce the name. "For best overall perform-
ance in math. . ." My heart pounded and I slid to the edge
of my seat. But, as she went on, I nearly choked. She didn't
call my name. Someone else won. Of course, Kate had
received the math award every year in high school. I
hadn't measured up once again.

One night I was in my room sitting at my desk when
Kate called from college. Ordinarily she didn't call for me,
but I happened to answer the phone.

"Hey, how's school?" she asked.

*Oh great. Here it was, her chance to compare. Her chance to
prove how much better she is,* I thought.

"Okay," I answered vaguely. She'd have to work a lot
harder to pull anything out of me.

"Did you do that experiment with the crucible of mag-
nesium and. . ."

"Yeah!" I replied, suddenly remembering the assignment. "It was cool. The flames burned so bright and there
was smoke everywhere."

"I remember that. That was fun," she said.

Wait a minute, I thought. *She didn't ask me about my grades.
Or brag about hers. What was going on? She wasn't comparing!
Yet. . .*

"And how's baseball?" she continued.

"Well, we're five and five. But we're playing pretty well."

"You're so good at sports. I hope I can get home soon to
see a game."

Again, that wasn't what I expected. Why didn't she tell

me that we should do better, win more?

We talked for a while longer. She told me a little about the classes she was taking, but mostly about her friends and going to shows and watching hockey games. I told her some stuff about school and sports.

By the time we hung up, I realized that we had had a good talk. And it wasn't all about who was better or smarter. Kate didn't bother comparing the two of us at all. I guess I was the only one who was stuck on doing that. She even thought some things I did were cool!

I settled back down at my desk and started to look over my homework. But wait—there was plenty more time before bed. First I'd play just one game of *NFL Blitz* on my Playstation. Kate probably wouldn't do it that way. But after all, I wasn't Kate. And that was just fine.

Andy Frezon, age 16
as told to Peggy Frezon

Reprinted by permission of Off the Mark and Mark Parisi. ©2007 Mark Parisi.

The Rosy Cheek

Courage is the price that life exacts for granting peace.

Amelia Earhart

It was the middle of winter and my brother and I, along with several other youths, had driven with our sponsors to Colorado for a ski trip. We had been having an amazing time staying up late, skiing the slopes, and driving our sponsors crazy.

At one of our meetings, the speaker had talked about turning the other cheek in order to defuse a volatile situation. Leaving the session, my friend Karla and I were walking down the hall when we ran into my brother Nathan and his friend Greg.

"Hey guys," my brother said, "you wanna get some pop and stuff from the gas station?"

"Sure," I glanced at Karla, who agreed. "How're we gonna get there?"

My brother dangled the keys.

"He gave them to you?" My face beamed. "Dad gave you the keys?"

"Yep."

"Cool, but how'd you convince him?"

"It's just down the block; he said to be right back."

Piling into the car, we headed out of the parking lot toward the gas station. Chatting about cool ski jumps and winding slopes, we were jolted back to reality as a car veered toward us, then squealed away.

"What's their problem?" I glanced at Karla, who shrugged her shoulders.

"Show-offs," Greg added.

We pulled into the gas station just as the other car did a one-eighty, jumped the curb, then pulled in front of us.

"Crazy drivers, what are they . . . " But I didn't have time to finish when a large boy yanked open the driver's door and grabbed my brother.

"You gave us the finger," the boy cursed, spilling forth a string of words I'd rather not repeat.

"No we didn't," my brother replied. His eyes darted toward us, pleading for help.

I could see he was scared. So were we. I looked at Greg. *Why wasn't he helping?* I thought. Karla didn't know what to do, either. I looked at Greg again. I then realized that if he spoke up, he'd get pounded, too. So I took a chance and opened the car door. *Maybe they wouldn't hurt a girl,* I thought.

The bully raised his fist. "I said you gave us the finger."

My brother shook his head no.

"You don't do that around here." The bully punched Nathan, shoving him to the ground.

"We didn't," my brother said.

The bully raised his fist. "I said you did, so you did." He hit my brother again, splitting his lip.

"But we didn't do it," I said, as I rushed to my big brother. I tried to hold back the tears. *Lord help us.*

But the bully ignored my pleas, pushing me back as he

grabbed my brother's shirt. Their eyes met. My brother's eyes were soft and full of kindness, the bullies filled with hate. For some reason Nathan remained silent, a strength greater than the bully's muscles.

"You did," the bully barked, throwing Nathan onto the concrete.

I rushed to my brother's side. *Why doesn't he fight back? Why doesn't he stick up for himself?* I glared at the bully, hatred building in my heart. I wanted to tear him apart but couldn't. Tears streamed down my hot face as I watched the bully approach my brother again. *Why wasn't anyone helping?*

The bully moved forward, but Nathan didn't budge. He raised his fist, but Nathan didn't flinch. With frustration building on the bully's face, he spat. "You're not worth it." He spun around and motioned his friends to leave. Within moments they were gone, the turmoil over.

"You okay?" I hugged my brother. "I thought he was going to kill you."

Nathan smiled. Getting to his feet, he wiped his oozing lip with his shirtsleeve. "Yeah, I'm fine." He never was much for words.

"Why didn't you fight back?" I asked.

"Didn't you listen to the message today?" Nathan said.

I shrugged. "Well, sort of."

"The speaker said to turn the other cheek, so that's what I did."

I stopped and smiled, appreciation for my brother rising in my heart. In a few short words, he had become my hero. No, not because he drove a car or was cool at school. He was my hero because of what he had *not* done that day.

My big brother didn't beat up the bad guy or bring him to justice; he saved me by taking the blows. He saved us by taking the scorn and ridicule so we wouldn't have to. In a world that prides itself on greatness, on being the best, the biggest, or the toughest, my big brother's weakness saved us that day. His weakness turned into a strength that could move mountains and block fists. He was my hero, bearing a superpower gained by turning a rosy cheek.

Arnita C. Wright

More Chicken Soup?

Many of the stories you have read in this book were submitted by readers like you who had read earlier Chicken Soup for the Soul books. We publish many Chicken Soup for the Soul books every year. We invite you to contribute a story to one of these future volumes.

Stories may be up to 1,200 words and must uplift or inspire. You may submit an original piece, something you have read, or your favorite quotation on your refrigerator door.

To obtain a copy of our submission guidelines and a listing of upcoming Chicken Soup books, please write, fax, or check our website.

Please send your submissions to:

Website: www.chickensoup.com
Chicken Soup for the Soul
P.O. Box 30880, Santa Barbara, CA 93130
fax: 805-563-2945

We will be sure that both you and the author are credited for your submission.

For information about speaking engagements, other books, audiotapes, workshops, and training programs, please contact any of our authors directly.

Supporting Others

The coauthors of *Chicken Soup for the Soul Celebrating Brothers & Sisters* have selected the LifeSkills Center for Leadership, based in Minneapolis, Minnesota, to receive a portion of the book's proceeds.

Character. Confidence. Choice. These are the core beliefs of The LifeSkills Center for Leadership. A nonprofit founded in 2001 by "Famous" Dave Anderson, the organization's objectives are to instill a sense of passion and hope and to empower youth to believe in themselves and to strive for their goals and dreams.

The LifeSkills Center for Leadership has been delivering life-changing training programs to build positive, responsible, and powerful leaders for today and for tomorrow. Upon completion of the training each youth begins the journey of looking at life's challenges as an opportunity to grow, ultimately becoming the person he or she was meant to be.

To learn more, please visit:
The LifeSkills Center for Leadership
1508 East Franklin Avenue, Suite 200
Minneapolis, MN 55404
Phone: 612-871-3883
Website: www.lifeskills-center.org
Website: www.pathtogreatness.com

Who Is Jack Canfield?

Jack Canfield is the cocreator and editor of the *Chicken Soup for the Soul* series, which *Time* magazine has called "the publishing phenomenon of the decade." The series now has more than 145 titles with over 100 million copies in print in forty-seven languages. Jack is also the coauthor of eight other bestselling books including *The Success Principles™: How to Get from Where You Are to Where You Want to Be, Dare to Win, The Aladdin Factor, You've Got to Read This Book,* and *The Power of Focus: How to Hit Your Business, Personal and Financial Targets with Absolute Certainty.*

Jack has recently developed a telephone coaching program and an online coaching program based on his most recent book *The Success Principles.* He also offers a seven-day Breakthrough to Success seminar every summer, which attracts 400 people from approximately fifteen countries around the world.

Jack is the CEO of Chicken Soup for the Soul Enterprises and the Canfield Training Group in Santa Barbara, California, and founder of the Foundation for Self-Esteem in Culver City, California. He has conducted intensive personal and professional development seminars on the principles of success for more than a million people in twenty-nine countries around the world. Jack is a dynamic keynote speaker and he has spoken to hundreds of thousands of others at more than 1,000 corporations, universities, professional conferences and conventions, and has been seen by millions more on national television shows such as *Oprah, Montel, The Today Show, Larry King Live, Fox and Friends, Inside Edition, Hard Copy,* CNN's *Talk Back Live, 20/20, Eye to Eye,* and the *NBC Nightly News* and the *CBS Evening News.* Jack was also a featured teacher in the hit film "The Secret."

Jack is the recipient of many awards and honors, including three honorary doctorates and a Guinness World Records Certificate for having seven books from the *Chicken Soup for the Soul* series appearing on *The New York Times* bestseller list on May 24, 1998.

To write to Jack or for inquiries about Jack as a speaker, his coaching programs, trainings or seminars, use the following contact information:

Jack Canfield
The Canfield Companies
P.O. Box 30880 • Santa Barbara, CA 93130
phone: 805-563-2935 • fax: 805-563-2945
E-mail: info4jack@jackcanfield.com
www.jackcanfield.com

Who Is Mark Victor Hansen?

In the area of human potential, no one is more respected than Mark Victor Hansen. For more than thirty years, Mark has focused solely on helping people from all walks of life reshape their personal vision of what's possible. His powerful messages of possibility, opportunity, and action have created powerful change in thousands of organizations and millions of individuals worldwide.

He is a sought-after keynote speaker, bestselling author, and marketing maven. Mark's credentials include a lifetime of entrepreneurial success and an extensive academic background. He is a prolific writer with many bestselling books, such as *The One Minute Millionaire, Cracking the Millionaire Code, How to Make the Rest of Your Life the Best of Your Life, The Power of Focus, The Aladdin Factor,* and *Dare to Win,* in addition to the Chicken Soup for the Soul series. Mark has had a profound influence on many people through his library of audios, videos, and articles in the areas of big thinking, sales achievement, wealth building, publishing success, and personal and professional development.

Mark is the founder of the MEGA Seminar Series. MEGA Book Marketing University and Building Your MEGA Speaking Empire are annual conferences where Mark coaches and teaches new and aspiring authors, speakers, and experts on building lucrative publishing and speaking careers. Other MEGA events include MEGA Info-Marketing and My MEGA Life.

He has appeared on *Oprah,* CNN, and *The Today Show.* He has been quoted in *Time, U.S. News & World Report, USA Today, The New York Times,* and *Entrepreneur.* In countless radio interviews, he has assured our planet's people that "you can easily create the life you deserve."

As a philanthropist and humanitarian, Mark works tirelessly for organizations such as Habitat for Humanity, American Red Cross, March of Dimes, Childhelp USA, and many others. He is the recipient of numerous awards that honor his entrepreneurial spirit, philanthropic heart, and business acumen. He is a lifetime member of the Horatio Alger Association of Distinguished Americans, an organization that honored Mark with the prestigious Horatio Alger Award for his extraordinary life achievements.

Mark Victor Hansen is an enthusiastic crusader of what's possible and is driven to make the world a better place.

Mark Victor Hansen & Associates, Inc.
P.O. Box 7665 • Newport Beach, CA 92658
phone: 949-764-2640 • fax: 949-722-6912
Website: www.markvictorhansen.com

Who Is Dahlynn McKowen?

Dahlynn McKowen is one of Chicken Soup for the Soul's most trusted coauthors. She, along with her husband, Ken, coauthored *Chicken Soup for the Fisherman's Soul* in May 2004. Dahlynn released *Chicken Soup for the Entrepreneur's Soul* in September 2006 and *Chicken Soup for the Soul in Menopause* in July 2007. The McKowens are currently creating a twelve-book travel series for Chicken Soup for the Soul Enterprises and Health Communications, Inc., a first for both companies, and are coauthoring many more Chicken Soup titles.

The McKowens stay active with their company, Publishing Syndicate, a small business that provides writing, ghostwriting, and editing services to publishers. They also offer a free monthly writing tips e-newsletter and have created an e-booklet series entitled "The Wow Principles." This series, which is sold via their website, focuses on aspects of writing for publication and profit. The McKowens also author other books each year, the most recent being *Best of California's Missions, Mansions, and Museums: Bringing the Golden State's Past Alive for Today's Travelers* (Wilderness Press).

Dahlynn is an established freelance writer with numerous book contracts and screenplays under production. Since selling her first feature article in 1987, she has produced over 2,000 works, including business features, B&B reviews, restaurant reviews, and travel articles. She is a well-known ghostwriter and has ghostwritten stories for a former U.S. president and more than two dozen Fortune 100 and 500 corporate founders and CEOs, as well as a few California governors.

Dahlynn loves spending as much time as she can with her ten-year-old son, Shawn, and teenage daughter, Lahre, who are both active in the family business (a professional photographer and a Chicken Soup cartoonist, respectively). She also loves discovering new travel destinations with hubby Ken. Needless to say, her life is not dull by any stretch of the imagination!

Dahlynn McKowen
Publishing Syndicate
P.O. Box 607
Orangevale, CA 95662
www.PublishingSyndicate.com

Who Is Ken McKowen?

Ken McKowen has been married to Chicken Soup coauthor Dahlynn McKowen for five years and helps manage their business, Publishing Syndicate. He retired a few years ago after working for the California State Parks system for thirty years.

Ken is a freelance writer and sold his first article to the travel section of a major newspaper in 1977—the same year his son Jason was born. Since then, his writing career has included several years as the head writer for the California State Parks' marketing and public relations office, penning feature articles for magazines and newspapers, writing brochure text, speeches, and advertising copy, as well as writing state park general plans and technical reports. During this same time, he was a freelancer selling outdoor and travel-related articles and photographs to magazines and newspapers. Ken has had several books published, including the highly acclaimed *The Longstreet Highroad Guide to the California Coast* and most recently coauthored with Dahlynn the *Best of California's Missions, Mansions and Museums* (Wilderness Press).

Ken's very successful efforts over the years in writing grant proposals and reviewing grant applications while working for state government led him to teaching the art of grant writing in numerous classes and seminars. He occasionally returns to his grant writer status to help local nonprofit groups who need grant funding.

Always seeking new areas of writing to explore, Ken is now writing songs and working on two novels and a screenplay. That's in addition to helping Dahlynn rear two children, fifteen-year-old Lahre and ten-year-old Shawn, while occasionally babysitting his eighteen-month-old grandson, Jake. In his few spare moments, Ken plays guitar, fishes, bicycles at least 100 miles each month, and builds custom furniture and kayaks.

Ken McKowen
Publishing Syndicate
P.O. Box 607
Orangevale, CA 95662
www.PublishingSyndicate.com

Contributors

Elena Aitken lives in Calgary, Alberta, with her husband and four-year-old twins. She keeps busy chasing her children as well as running her own copywriting business, Ink Blot Communications. She is currently finishing her first novel. She can be reached at www.inkblotcommunications.ca or elena@inkblotcommunications.ca.

Diana M. Amadeo is an award-winning author, a busy wife, mother, former registered nurse, volunteer, and freelance writer. Her 400-plus publications include books, anthologies, magazine features, and newspaper articles. She loves traveling and creating memories with her family.

Linda Apple is an inspirational/motivational speaker for women's retreats and conferences. She speaks for Stonecroft Ministries. She also conducts workshops for writers' groups and conferences on writing creative nonfiction. She is published in nine *Chicken Soup for the Soul* books and recently completed her first novel. Contact Linda at psalm10218@cox.net.

Aaron Bacall has graduate degrees in organic chemistry as well as in educational administration and supervision from New York University. Three of his cartoons are featured in the permanent collection at the Harvard Business School's Baker Library. He continues to create and sell his cartoons. Reach him at abacall@msn.com.

Joe Beaulieu is currently a junior in high school. He likes writing, reading, music, playing guitar, and watching movies.

JoAnne Bennett lives in the Pacific Northwest with her husband and three daughters. She loves sharing her true-life narratives with vivid, colorful descriptions and a fresh style. Her most recent writing accomplishments include articles in *Children Today* and *Sasee Magazine*. Please e-mail her at Storiesbyjb@yahoo.com.

Cynthia Borris is the award-winning author of *No More Bobs*, a quirky misadventure. She resides in California and is a frequent *Chicken Soup for the Soul* contributor. A humor columnist and inspirational speaker, she is working on her next novel, *To Serve Duck*. Please contact Cynthia at cynthiaborris@juno.com or www.cynthiaborris.com.

Renie Burghardt is a freelance writer. Her work has been published in magazines and many anthologies, including five *Chicken Soup for the Soul* books. She lives in the country and loves nature, animals, and spending time with family and friends. E-mail her at renie_burghardt@yahoo.com.

Salvatore Buttaci is a retired English teacher, first published in the *New York News* at age sixteen. His poems, letters, and stories have been published in *The New York Times, Newsday, USA Today, The Writer, Cats Magazine,* and elsewhere. His recent book, *A Dusting of Star Fall,* is currently available. E-mail him at sambpoet@yahoo.com.

Glen A. Carlsen is a new at-home dad after working for twenty years restoring furniture at the Sagamore Resort in northern New York. He has a bachelor's degree in theater from Potsdam College and one published book, and was a humor columnist for a weekly paper. E-mail him at g3carl@localnet.com.

Barbara Elliott Carpenter is the author of *The Starlight Trilogy,* books that are capturing the hearts of readers across the country and are available at bookstores and on-line sellers. Her website is www.barbaraelliottcarpenter.com, or e-mail her at bjlogger2@aol.com.

Lucile C. Cason lives near Atlanta, Georgia, where she enjoys writing creative nonfiction, fiction, poetry, and memories from a lifetime as a registered nurse. Her work has been published in *The Rocking Chair Reader: Family Gathering, Cup of Comfort for Nurses,* and *Small Town Life* magazine.

Emily Parke Chase and her brother Richard share a love of writing. Emily is the author of five books, including *Why Say No When My Hormones Say Go?* She speaks to thousands of teens each year about relationship issues. Visit her at emilychase.com.

Karna Converse has as many memories of winning ping-pong games as well as losing them to her brother, and she foresees the same happening during ping-pong games with her children. A freelance writer, she lives in Storm Lake, Iowa, with her husband and their three children. Please contact her at conversekj@iw.net.

Linda Cook lives and writes from redwood country in the northwest corner of California. She enjoys reading, gardening, garage sales, and anything chocolate. Married and the mother of sons, Linda finds the men in her life provide writing inspiration and keep her days filled with joy and laughter. Contact Linda at readme.linda@gmail.com.

Mike Cope is a freelance cartoonist and multimedia designer from Stoney Creek, Ontario. His cartoons have been published in books and magazines by Reader's Digest Canada. He's currently aspiring to create a syndicated comic strip. Mike enjoys teaching cartooning to kids and adults. For more information visit http://copetoons.com.

Lyndsey D'Arcangelo is a full-time copywriter at the *Buffalo News* and a creative writer on the side. She has written numerous short stories, poems, and columns and has completed two novels. She is currently working on her third novel. You can visit her on the Web at www.dreamaloftydream.com.

Donna Dawkin spent twenty years as a classical chef. A lifestyle change came with a move to the west coast of British Columbia. Donna feeds the flame of her imagination by creating spectacular fiction. She enjoys her family, nature, digital photography, and living in the moment. E-mail her at donnadawkin@hotmail.com.

Lucille Engro DiPaolo resides in Plymouth Meeting, Pennsylvania. In 2005, her first book, *As Walked With My Mother*, was published. Her website is www.caringforparentswithalzheimers.com. Mrs. DiPaolo was employed by the Colonial School District for fourteen years. She enjoys traveling, reading, and spending time with family and friends.

Terri Duncan received her bachelor's, master's, and specialist's degrees in education from Augusta State University. She is currently a graduation coach in Evans, Georgia, and is also a devoted wife and the mother of two delightful teenagers. Her dream is to have published a full-length book suitable for children.

Theresa J. Elders works in Colville, WA, promoting healthcare occupations. With the Peace Corps, she served in Belize, Dominican Republic, and Seychelles, and was a health program and training specialist in Washington, DC. She holds an MSW from UCLA, receiving the 2006 UCLA Community Service Award. E-mail her at telders@hotmail.com.

Norma Favor currently lives in British Columbia and vacations in Idaho during the summer. She has been published in *Chicken Soup for the Grandma's Soul* and *Chicken Soup for the Shopper's Soul*, and also in *Classic Christmas* and *A Cup of Comfort Weddings*, both by Adams Media.

Lisa Davenport Freeman received her B.A. and M.A. from Brigham Young University (BYU) and taught French at BYU and the University of Virginia. She lives in Utah with her husband, the prolific author Robert Freeman, and three awesome stepchildren. Her next project is a travel book about France. E-mail her at lisadfreeman@yahoo.com

Peggy Frezon is a full-time freelance writer from New York. She is a regular contributor to *Guideposts, Sweet 16, Angels on Earth* and other magazines and anthologies. She enjoys spending time with her husband, Mike, and her son and daughter, who often share their brother and sister stories. Contact her at http://peggyfrezon.googlepages.com.

Leticia Gómez is the CEO/Founder of Savvy Literary Services, a full-service literary agency specializing in the Latino book market. She is also a freelance book editor and literary translator. Leticia Gómez resides in Woodlands, Texas, with her husband, a structural engineer, and two children, Zakaria, seven, and Yasmine, five.

Nancy Kay Grace lives in Springdale, Arkansas, where her husband, Rick, is a senior pastor. She is a CLASS speaker and freelance writer with several magazine credits. Nancy is working on a book on self-esteem and a manuscript with her husband on partnership marriage. Please visit her at www.nancygrace.com.

Wendy Greenley followed her brother out the window of their home in Princeton Junction, New Jersey. She lives in Pennsylvania with her husband and sons where she enjoys watching her boys' own first leaps. Still leaping herself, Wendy is pursuing a career writing for children. E-mail her at wgreenley@att.net.

Jonny Hawkins dedicates the cartoons in this book to his three sisters, Lisa, Becky, and Ronelle, and to his brother Joey, without whom his cartooning career would not be possible. His cartoon-a-day calendars and books can be found online and in stores or by contacting jonny hawkins2nz@yahoo.com.

Julie Henry received her B.A., with honors, from Carleton University, Ottawa, Canada, in 1996. A full-time writer and mother of three, Julie enjoys boating, reading, and spending time with her family and friends. She is currently working on her first novel. Please e-mail her at sj_henry@sympatico.ca.

Laurie Heron's life is provided focus by Kamryn, Quinn, Jed, Xavier, and Sydni, as they create chaos, joy, frustration, and hope. Laurie also writes grant applications for non-profit organizations while pursuing her master's degree in public administration. She would love any comments at laurieheron@hotmail.com.

Miriam Hill is coauthor of *Fabulous Florida* and a frequent contributor to *Chicken Soup for the Soul* books. She's been published in the *Christian Science Monitor, Grit, St. Petersburg Times,* and *Poynter Online.* Miriam's manuscript received honorable mention for inspirational writing in the 75th Annual *Writer's Digest* writing competition.

Renee Hixson is a freelance writer and full-time homemaker who hopes to finish her first book this spring. Her secret dream is to be a stand-up comedian. Please e-mail her at rhixson@telus.net.

Caroleah Johnson started her writing career after thirty-four years of practicing dental hygiene. This is her second Chicken Soup story. She writes inspirational material, produces her church's newsletter, and is working on a novel. She and her husband live in Northern California. Please e-mail her at caroleah@gmail.com.

Vivian M. Johnson has one daughter and three sons. Although she has long been an avid reader, writing is a new adventure for her. She currently lives in Texas with her husband and three sons. Content being a stay-at-home mom, she admits to having aspirations of becoming a writer. E-mail her at Vivian21470@yahoo.com.

Susan Karas resides on Long Island in New York. She began focusing on her writing career once her children, Christopher and Lindsay, were off on their own. She and her husband, Bruce, operate a successful business and enjoy nature and gardening in their free time. Please e-mail her at SueZFoofer@aol.com.

Joe Lair, his wife, Tanya, and their three children live in Bozeman, Montana, one of the most beautiful places on earth. They enjoy outdoor activities, especially skiing and hiking. Joe loves to write and speak, and his story "Fish Tacos" appeared in the *Chicken Soup for the Fisherman's Soul*. Contact him at www.josephtlair.com.

Margaret Lang is a published author of over twenty stories, many in *Chicken Soup for the Soul* books. She teaches Christian studies to women's and childrens' groups in the U.S., Thailand, and Australia, her favorite topic being intimacy with the Lord. She loves to spend time with her granddaughters in Colorado.

Lauren Manekin was raised in Baltimore, Maryland, and has been leading active travel vacations around the world with Backroads since graduation in 2002 from Goucher College of Maryland. Her stories find their way to computers around the world and she plans to eventually write a book.

Melanie Marks was born and raised in California. She is married to a naval officer and blessed with three amazingly terrific kids. She writes books for children and young adults. You can e-mail Melanie at bymelaniemarks@comcast.net.

Lynn Marshall is a researcher for the northwest bureau of the *Los Angeles Times*, based in Seattle. In her free time she writes about food and travel in the Northwest. She enjoys kayaking and spending time with her husband, her two dogs, and her three cats.

Glady Martin used to write just for her personal use, but soon came to see how she was expressing herself openly to others through her writing. Her philosophy is that life is an amazing adventure when expressed through words of laughter. E-mail her at gladymartin320@hotmail.com.

Megan Martin lives in Columbia, Missouri, with her husband of twenty-seven years. She enjoys being a mother to her two children, who are out of the nest and doing well. She has enjoyed being a writer all of her life, particularly when writing romance novels, short stories, and children's books.

Jay Max lives on Long Island with his family who are a constant source of inspiration and humor. Currently working on several creative projects, he is always looking for new illustration opportunities. Please drop him a line at JayMax@hotmail.com for links to his online portfolios, or just to say hello.

Michelle L. McCormick earned her B.S. at the University of North Florida. She found her calling while studying for her master's in journalism at the University of South Florida. Her passion is in the Christian writers' field, and she hopes to write for young adults. Please e-mail her at michellemccormick2@hotmail.com.

Kari Mills is a freshman at Northeast Community College, pursuing business. She coaches volleyball for a team in Corinth, Mississippi. Kari enjoys playing the piano and volleyball, and writing short essays. Please e-mail her at airmarsis@yahoo.com.

Kimberly Misra lives in western Massachusetts with her husband and three children. She is a freelance writer and a homeschooling mom who also enjoys reading, traveling, and gardening. She can be reached at kmmsra@gmail.com.

Tina O'Reilly is a freelance writer who resides in Warwick, Rhode Island, with her husband, three children, and two labs. She loves to hear from readers. Contact her at seaswept68@aol.com.

Cindy Ovard is an award-winning writer and has been writing stories since she was young. She received her bachelor's degree from San Diego Mesa College. Cindy loves family vacations and making memories. You can e-mail her at cindyovard@hotmail.com.

Jeanne Pallos is the author of several published articles for adults and children. She is a board member for the Orange County Christian Writers Fellowship in Southern California. Jeanne lives in Laguna Niguel, California, with her husband, Andrew. They are the proud parents of two adult children.

Mark Parisi's "Off the Mark" comic, syndicated since 1987, is distributed by United Media. Mark's humor also graces greeting cards, T-shirts, calendars, magazines, newsletters, and books. Check out: offthemark.com. Lynn is his wife/business partner. Their daughter, Jen, contributes with inspiration (as do three cats).

Tommy Polk is an award-winning songwriter living in Nashville, Tennessee, and Clarksdale, Mississippi, where he is owner of bigpink guesthouse.com. His songs have been recorded by Martina McBride, Diamond Rio, Carolyn Dawn Johnson, Crystal Gayle, and others.

Robert Raina studied art at the University of Massachusetts at Amherst. He is a cartoonist and has written and illustrated several children's books.

Robert is the president and owner of an entertainment company in western Massachusetts (bobrainadj.com). Contact him at robertraina@cox.net. His writing and art work can be viewed at bobrainawriting.com.

Kellie Randle and husband, Jeff, own a public relations firm in Sacramento, California. A UCLA alumnus, Kellie previously worked in politics and taught elementary school. She enjoys photography, writing, skiing, and travel. Kellie travels with her husband and three children, with Japan and Cuba as the latest highlights. E-mail her at Krandle@surewest.net.

Lahre Shiflet's cartoons have been featured in six Chicken Soup books. Besides drawing, she also likes to sing, model, and act, as well as write original music on her Mac computer and then perform her music. A teenager, Lahre's favorite thing to do is hang out with her friends.

Shawn Shiflet is in fourth grade. When he grows up, he wants to design Lamborghini automobiles in Italy. Shawn also likes to cook and play video games with his mom, Dahlynn McKowen.

Kimberly Sowell has reached thousands through her high-energy messages, connecting with women through her funny stories of everyday life and love. Her fresh perspectives in applying the Bible to life have drawn many women to make life-changing commitments to live as Christ did. Learn about her ministry of speaking and writing at www. KimberlySowell.net.

Joyce Stark lives in northeast Scotland and has recently retired from local government. She is now working on a travel book to encourage people to drive the U.S., exploring small towns and backroads as well as main attractions. You can contact her at joric.stark@virgin.net.

Jean Stewart writes about family, travel, and history from her Mission Viejo, California, home. She's been married forty-six years and is the mother of twin daughters, the grandmother of two, and a sister to one brother who lives in Georgia. Her stories are in Chicken Soup books as well as other anthologies, newspapers, and magazines.

Melanie Stiles is a writer, speaker, and award-winning poet. Her life interests include ministering to women on self-esteem. Melanie spends her free time playing with the light of her life—her granddaughter, Maile. Visit her website, www.melaniestiles.com, to learn more.

R. J. Thesman is a writer who specializes in nonfiction and devotionals, although an occasional foray into fiction stirs the creative soup. She enjoys research, working with people, gardening, and petting cats.

Paulie Tietz's primary career is wife and mother. Children raised, she completed her education with an M.A. in counseling psychology and has worked as a professional counselor for fifteen years. She enjoys sewing, crafting, drawing, and riding her motorcycle, *Lady Rebel*. Her writing began with stories for her grandchildren. Contact her at tietz@eods.com.

Sandra Toney is an award-winning author of eight books on cat care and behavior. She has had hundreds of articles published during her thirteen-year freelance career. Sandra has a flourishing photography business as well. She lives in Indiana with her husband, Ray, and three cats. E-mail her at sandratoney@petwriter.net.

Cristy Trandahl is a former teacher and writer for the nation's leading student progress monitoring company. Today she works as a freelance writer and home educates her six children. Cristy's stories are included in numerous, nationally distributed anthologies. Check out Cristy's website at www.cristytrandahl.com.

Kathy Shiels Tully wrote an op-ed about Leap Day, February 29th, in 1992. Taking her article's advice, she proposed another Leap Day op-ed in 1996, getting a byline, TV appearance, husband, and later, daughters Bridget and Katie. Currently, she is writing a book on sabbaticals. Contact her at Kathytully@comcast.net.

Fay Ulanoff is a former New Yorker who now resides in Loveland, Colorado. She is a ventriloquist and puppeteer. Her love of the written word focuses mainly on children's literature and is reflected in her productions. She is currently working on a young adult novella. E-mail her at lilfaith@comcast.net.

Sheila Vincent-Bright, reared in Lexington, Missouri, comes from a long line of storytellers. In 2005 she decided to write about the adventures she and her brother shared growing up. Her mother taught her to love God, family, and country. She enjoys attending church, her family, writing, old movies, and being outdoors.

Beverly Watson is a graduate of Georgetown University's School of Foreign Service and Stanford University's Law School. She has lived and worked in various countries throughout Africa and Latin America, focusing on international development, education, and legal issues. She currently lives in Washington, D.C.

Jane Wiatrek is a retired educator who began as a teacher and then became a school administrator. She and her husband, Ben, live in Poth, Texas. She enjoys reading, writing, and spending time with her three grown sons, Grayson, Jared, and Cory, her brother, Joe, and other family and friends. Contact Jane at janedw3@yahoo.com.

Arthur Wiknik, Jr. is a Vietnam veteran of the battle for Hamburger Hill and had his wartime memoir, *Nam Sense,* published in 2005. He has written a wide variety of articles for publication, including three previous Chicken Soup stories. Arthur frequently shares his wartime experiences at schools and civic organizations. Contact him at www.namsense.com.

Nolyn Wilson has dreamt of being an author since she was young. She enjoys writing, signing, performing, running, church camps, and going on mission trips. She spends most of her free time writing, hanging out with friends, instant messaging, or talking on the phone.

Arnita C. Wright is the author of *The Journey, The Stone* (2007 release), and several published short stories. A wife, mother, and award-winning author, Arnita has a degree from Bethany Bible College in California. She lives with her husband and daughter in Topeka, Kansas. Visit her at www.myspace.com/faithwriter or at www.arnitacwright.org.

Patsy Zettler received her master of arts in media communications from Webster University in St. Louis, Missouri, in 2004. As a columnist for the *St. Charles County Suburban Journal,* Patsy focuses on domestic humor with one of her favorite subjects being life with teens. Please e-mail her at pzettler@mail.win.org.

Unforgettable Memories

Remember when_____

_____

_____

_____

_____

_____

_____

_____

_____

Remember when_____

_____

_____

_____

_____

_____

_____

_____

_____

Unforgettable Memories

Remember when_____

_____

_____

_____

_____

_____

_____

_____

Remember when_____

_____

_____

_____

_____

_____

_____

_____

_____

Chicken Soup for the Sister's Soul 2

Celebrating Love and Laughter Throughout Our Lives

**Jack Canfield, Mark Victor Hansen,
Patty Aubery and Kelly Mitchell Zimmerman**

Code #5512 • $14.95

Also Available

Chicken Soup African American Soul
Chicken Soup African American Woman's Soul
Chicken Soup Breast Cancer Survivor's Soul
Chicken Soup Bride's Soul
Chicken Soup Caregiver's Soul
Chicken Soup Cat Lover's Soul
Chicken Soup Christian Family Soul
Chicken Soup College Soul
Chicken Soup Couple's Soul
Chicken Soup Dieter's Soul
Chicken Soup Dog Lover's Soul
Chicken Soup Entrepreneur's Soul
Chicken Soup Expectant Mother's Soul
Chicken Soup Father's Soul
Chicken Soup Fisherman's Soul
Chicken Soup Girlfriend's Soul
Chicken Soup Golden Soul
Chicken Soup Golfer's Soul, Vol. I, II
Chicken Soup Horse Lover's Soul, Vol. I, II
Chicken Soup Inspire a Woman's Soul
Chicken Soup Kid's Soul, Vol. I, II
Chicken Soup Mother's Soul, Vol. I, II
Chicken Soup Parent's Soul
Chicken Soup Pet Lover's Soul
Chicken Soup Preteen Soul, Vol. I, II
Chicken Soup Scrapbooker's Soul
Chicken Soup Sister's Soul, Vol. I, II
Chicken Soup Shopper's Soul
Chicken Soup Soul, Vol. I-VI
Chicken Soup at Work
Chicken Soup Sports Fan's Soul
Chicken Soup Teenage Soul, Vol. I-IV
Chicken Soup Woman's Soul, Vol. I, II